HISTORY TEACHERS
IN THE MAKING

HISTORY TEACHERS IN THE MAKING
Professional Learning

Anna Pendry and Chris Husbands
& James Arthur and Jon Davison

Open University Press
Buckingham · Philadelphia

Open University Press
Celtic Court
22 Ballmoor
Buckingham
MK18 1XW

email: enquiries@openup.co.uk
world wide web: http://www.openup.co.uk

and

325 Chestnut Street
Philadelphia, PA19106, USA

First Published 1998

A catalogue record of this book is available from the British Library

ISBN   0 335 19825 2 (pb)   0 335 19826 0 (hb)

Library of Congress Cataloging-in-Publication Data
Pendry, Anna, 1954–
     Professional learning: history teachers in the making/Anna
 Pendry and Chris Husbands & James Arthur and Jon Davison.
     p.   cm.
 Includes bibliographical references and index.
     ISBN 0–335–19826–0. – ISBN 0–335–19825–2 (pbk.)
     1. History – Study and teaching (Higher)   2. History – Study and
 teaching (Higher) – Great Britain.   3. History – Methodology.
 I. Husbands, Christopher T.   II. Title.
 D16.2.P385   1998
 907.1'1 – dc21   97–47456
                                                                             CIP

Typeset by Graphicraft Typesetters Ltd, Hong Kong
Printed in Great Britain by St Edmundsbury Press Ltd, Bury St Edmunds

CONTENTS

PREFACE

This book explores the development of history teachers, and therefore of history teaching. At the core of the book are two linked notions. The first is that we regard history teaching as a relatively complex intellectual exercise, which makes significant demands on the expertise and professionalism of history teachers. We are interested to explore the nature of this expertise and this professionalism, and to offer some thoughts and ideas on how it might be developed. We hope that these ideas will be directly useful to new, student teachers and their mentors in schools and higher education, as well as supporting experienced teachers in developing their effectiveness. Like other researchers, we argue that effective development of classroom expertise depends on defining, and helping practitioners to articulate, the nature of classroom expertise and some of its current limitations. The second notion is to do with the nature of history as a discipline and as a school subject. We believe history teaching to be relatively complex because classrooms are, almost by definition, complex places, but we also argue that history teaching is complex because of the nature of the discipline. We do not regard history teaching as being about the transmission of 'content' nor the acquisition of decontextualized 'skills'; equally, we do not believe that history teaching is in some reductive way a vehicle of 'political education' and 'values', nor predominantly concerned with the development of 'historical concepts'. History teaching is about *all* of these things, and one of the complexities with which history teachers and history learners have to deal is the nature of the discipline and the complexity of the ideas which underpin it. For example, the teaching of, say, the Industrial Revolution involves the transmission of a good deal of 'factual' knowledge, about inventions and their impact and the dates of their impact on different industrial sectors, but it also, inevitably, involves the development of skills in deciphering the fragmentary nature of the evidence, unlocking and understanding the relationship between longer-term and short-term causes and consequences, economic, social and technological issues and, inescapably, the moral and value-laden questions of the impact of the Industrial Revolution on the lives of those who lived through it and, like ourselves, inherit the world it created. History teaching is, in part, about making appropriate and meaningful selections from this complexity for learners. This book does not set out to unpack all of that complexity, but it does attempt to contribute to the development of history teachers who are capable of articulating this complexity.

The original proposal for the book was developed by James Arthur and Jon Davison, and the book was substantially written by Anna Pendry and Chris Husbands. In particular, the chapters in Parts 1 and 3 were authored collaboratively by Anna and Chris. The chapters in section 2 were written by James and Jon and then edited by Chris and Anna.

We have accumulated numerous debts in writing the book, and we would like to express our thanks to colleagues at Warwick and Oxford, in particular to Katharine Burn. Most of all, however, we would like to thank those history teachers and student teachers in Oxfordshire, East Anglia, Coventry and Warwickshire with whom we have been privileged to work closely, and whose classroom practices have both generated many of our examples and underpin the arguments we advance.

Anna Pendry
Chris Husbands

1

LEARNING IN HISTORY CLASSROOMS

Three history lessons

Lesson 1: Nineteenth-century parliamentary reform Year 9, mixed ability

The 30 pupils enter and take their places in rows. The teacher, remaining seated, takes the register. Pupils answer to their names in turn. The teacher comments on a piece of homework that has been returned, telling the pupils that their work had generally been completed satisfactorily but drawing attention to the need for some of them to finish the work. The teacher stands, and distributes information sheets on nineteenth-century parliamentary reform to the pupils.

'Remember what we've been looking at: protest and reform. What kinds of thing do we mean when we think about reform?', the teacher asks the pupils. A pupil responds, 'Is a reform a peaceful protest?' The teacher re-directs the pupils by asking, 'When something is reformed what happens?', and a pupil replies that, 'It changes.' The teacher takes up this idea, saying, 'Yes, it changes, and at this time we are looking mainly at reforms in parliament, and the charts you were filling in were on parliamentary reform, changes in parliament. Now what kinds of things changed?' A third pupil responds, 'Who can vote.' 'Yes', says the teacher, 'so when we use this magical word reform, that's what we're talking about, and, yes, it's slow, often, and usually a peaceful change. What you've got on your worksheet is about a very important change in 1832 looked at from different angles. What you have on the right-hand side are three quotations said by the three people on the left – William Cobbett, The Duke of Wellington and Robert Peel. Your task is to match the quotation to the person. We'll look through the quotations because it's nineteenth-century language.'

He reads the quotations to the class asking pupils what each means, repeating key phrases and then rephrasing the answers for the class. The third quotation includes the phrase, 'We shall have one of the worst despotisms'. 'Now that word despotism', says the teacher, 'does anyone know what it means?' There is a pause. 'Does anyone know what a tyrant is?' There is no response. 'Let me see if I can give you an example. Hitler in Germany, Stalin in Russia, people who have total power to do what they like: they're despots.' He resumes reading. This time he stops at the phrase, 'We shall have a mob of demagogues' and comments, 'That word, demagogue, it's a really nice word! A demagogue is a person who really excites large crowds of people and says he will give them what they want. It can be a really dangerous thing, can't it?' This last sentence is spoken expansively, the teacher gesturing like a demagogue. He resumes reading, ' "a mob of demagogues, not wise or prudent men . . .". Right, now, you need to read the information about the three people and match each one to the quotation. It should only take a few minutes.'

We are now ten minutes into the lesson and pupils work on their task, with the teacher circulating. After a couple of minutes he says, 'If you think you have got the answer, write down beside it what you think told you what the answer was, how you knew it was the answer. That's the really important bit.' He continues to move around the classroom, checking work for three or four minutes, before returning to the centre front of the room. Leaning on his chair, he asks, 'So, who would like to tell me who said the first quotation.' A pupil responds 'Cobbett'. 'Yes, good, it was Cobbett, writing in the *Political Register* in the 1820s. Now can anyone tell me why you chose Cobbett?' The teacher collects pupils' reasons using their responses to indicate key issues, and making links with previous work, using his commentary to set Cobbett's views in the context of social change during the Industrial Revolution. After going through each quotation and assigning an author, the teacher focuses on key historical issues. 'Are you surprised we have these three different points of view? After all, conditions were the same, conditions were not good, working people did not have the vote, so why were there different points of view? Lee thinks he has an answer.'

Lesson 2: Second World War, Year 9, lower ability group

The 26 pupils enter the room and take their seats around tables arranged so that groups of four can face each other. After taking the register the teacher says, 'World War II; what comes to mind when I say that?' There is a pause. 'What comes into your head if I say Second World War?' The pupils begin to call out words and phrases. 'Trenches' – 'Hitler' – 'Germans' – 'Dead bodies' – 'Tanks' – 'Dad's Army' – 'Rationing' – 'Blitz' – 'Evacuation' – 'Children' – 'Spitfires' – 'Churchill' – '1914' – 'Poland' – 'It'll be over by Christmas' – 'Jews'. As the pupils call out, the teacher logs the words exactly as said on the board. As soon as there is a pause, she says, 'OK, so, we've got lots of ideas about the Second World War. What we're going to do is find out more about it, and then we'll come back to your words and see what you think about them.'

She begins to distribute to pairs of pupils A3 sheets, which have on them a series of pictorial images of the war. As she moves round the room, she tells the pupils what she would like them to do. 'Look carefully at each of the pictures. Jot down in your rough books what that tells you about the war. You might like to think about any people in the pictures, where those people are, what sort of state they are in, any weapons you can see. I'll give you about five minutes and then we'll see how you are getting on.' She stands at the front watching for a few moments as the pupils begin their task. She spots two pupils looking rather bewildered and goes over and quietly reiterates the instructions. The five minutes pass, but pupils are still engrossed. She leaves them a little longer. When she feels that off-task conversation levels begin to rise, she returns to the front of the room and draws the class together.

'So, who were the people in the pictures? Tony, who did you get?' He replies 'Ladies. Soldiers. There was a child in that one [points to the pictures].' The teacher asks if anyone has anything to add, and one pupil comments that the picture on the left seems to be of important people. The teacher then directs the pupils' attention to the apparent location of each of the pictures. The pupils identify London, 'somewhere abroad', and 'a desert'. The teacher continues with the questioning, establishing with the pupils that a wide range of people and places were involved in the war. Then she says, 'some writers have used the words "total war" to describe the Second World War. Now, what we're going to do is to see if we agree with them.'

Lesson 3: Tudor social structure, Year 8, mixed ability

The 28 pupils enter the room, and take their seats in rows. After calling the register, the teacher says, 'Now, today we are going to be moving around the room quite a lot, so the first thing you need to do is to move the tables quietly. I'll tell you what I want you to do.' He organizes the movement of tables and then asks pupils to arrange their chairs in a circle, and take their seats. From the front of the room, he introduces the lesson.

'Over the last few weeks we have been doing some work on how people in the sixteenth century lived and worked. Today you are going to find out how they felt about each other, how society was organized. I am going to give you a card. It's very important that at no point you show your card to anyone else. It's your card, and it's secret. Your card will tell you two things: it will give you a number from 1 to 28, and a part that you will play. For example, number 1 is Queen Elizabeth I. You know that she was the most important person in the country! Number 2 is Lord Burghley, who was Queen Elizabeth's most important adviser. Number 28 is Simon Scroggs, who is a poor, homeless beggar. The person who has card number 1 is the most important person in the room – but of course, only he or she will know they've got card number 1. The person with card number 28 is the least important person in the room – and only he or she knows that they are number 28. If you have a number between 1 and 28, then you are somewhere in between, and the nearer your number is to number 1, the more important you are! So, I'll hand out your cards now, and I want you to read about yourself – remember to keep it secret – and decide how you think you are likely to behave to others. You'll then have five minutes to stand up, and move about the room, playing your part, but not telling anyone else what your number is!' The teacher distributes the cards and the pupils read the descriptions, giggling as they find out their roles. Once the cards are distributed the teacher tells the pupils they can move around the room. For five minutes they do so, some bowing, some begging, some haughtily.

The teacher claps his hands for attention and asks the class to return to their seats. He now begins to 'decode' the roles. 'So, Amarjit, who do *you* think had card number one?' Amarjit points to Helen. The teacher asks others if they agree, and Helen is quickly identified as Queen Elizabeth I. Then the teacher asks pupils to identify number 28. Again, agreement is quickly reached as Paul is identified. Helen and Paul are asked to stand at each end of one of the classroom walls, and the teacher now asks pupils if they can suggest who should go at what point between them. After much discussion and debate, the class and teacher agree a hierarchy and the class are lined up. The teacher stands in front of the line and begins to make some teaching points. He asks all those whose roles involved landowning to identify themselves, then all those with roles in the church, then all those playing female roles and so on. Gradually, the class builds up an idea of Tudor social structure from the activity, before they are asked to sit down again. Now the teacher gives out a further piece of paper containing quotations from William Harrison's 1577 *Description of England*, and he asks the class to read it in pairs and to compare Harrison's account with the role-playing exercise they have undertaken.

Unpacking learning in history

The complexity of history classrooms

What do these three lessons tell us about teaching and learning in history? Perhaps the first observation to make is that all three lessons are complex, and merit close analysis. This complexity arises from a number of sources. The first is to do with the nature of the historical content of the lessons, of the material being taught. The nature of 'reform' in early nineteenth-century Britain, the concept of 'total war', and Tudor social structure all involve relatively abstract ideas and the acquisition of a substantial amount of contextual knowledge. Like many other topics that form the staple of history in secondary schools they are content areas that pose significant challenges for teachers to make accessible and for pupils across the ability range to understand (Fines 1987). The ways in which the teachers, and their pupils, respond to the demands of the material are central to understanding the nature of teaching and learning in the three lessons.

The second element of complexity follows from this. Given the nature of the material, the composition of the classes and a host of other contextual features, the teachers in these lessons were faced with a large number of planning decisions to make when preparing the lesson and then a further range of decisions to make in adjusting their intentions in the light of what actually happened in the lesson: the responses pupils gave to the brainstorming activity in the first lesson, or the question and answer session in the second lesson (Clark and Yinger 1979; John 1994; Pendry 1994, 1997). In addition to these largely content-related decisions, there were other decisions that teachers were required to make in order to run the lessons. The lessons had to be related to the content and assessment demands of the national curriculum and examination syllabuses, and they had to be planned in the light of the available resources, both material and less tangible, such as the teaching time available and the lesson length (Morine-Dershimer 1979). Some of the decisions to approach the content in particular ways were perhaps made for situational reasons: to exercise effective classroom control, or to ensure the involvement of particular pupils at particular stages of the lesson. In planning for, and working in, the classroom, teachers have a great deal to think about in addition to teaching, which itself is complex enough.

The lessons were complex, finally, because of the complexity of learning, and, in classrooms, the number of different learners involved (Postlethwaite 1993). In each of these three lessons there were at least 25 pupils, all with different preferred ways of working, and different perceptions. One task for the teacher was to establish classroom procedures that not only made the lesson content *in principle* accessible, but ensured that it was accessible to those pupils in those lessons. In each lesson the teachers negotiated hundreds of individual encounters with pupils, adjusting language and style to each one (Calderhead 1988). But there are other demands for pupils too. Working in history classrooms is not, for them, just about learning history: there are the different assumptions and expectations of *these* teachers to adapt to, and the different dynamics of this teaching group. Some recent research suggests that 'learning' is relatively low on pupils' lists of priorities as an activity that takes place at school: school may be where you socialize with your friends, exchange news about the latest fashions and films. In many cases, learning about Second World War, or nineteenth-century reform or sixteenth-century society is not high on pupils' priorities (Rudduck 1996). If we want to understand, and contribute to the development of, history teaching in schools, then the starting point has to be classrooms like these, in all their complexity, and the questions we can pose on the basis of the classrooms.

The goals of history lessons

The following general observations relate to what the teachers were trying to achieve. What is striking is the variety of identifiable short-term goals represented in these three lessons (Gudmundsdottir 1991). The teacher in the first lesson appears to have been concerned with developing pupils' understanding of both an historical process (the process of political reform in early nineteenth-century Britain) and the substantive concepts used by historians (Lee 1991) to describe the process. In the second lesson, the teacher's main goal would appear to be to involve pupils in developing and testing a hypothesis about the concept of 'total war': is the concept of 'total war' a useful one for historians? The goals of the third lesson appear to have been different. Although the lesson was firmly located in the context of particular historical content, the teacher appears to have had rather more affective goals for pupil understanding in the lesson, enhancing pupils' understanding by giving them an opportunity to enjoy themselves and to learn through imagined experience (Barker 1978; Neelands 1993).

This discussion of teachers' goals focuses largely on the immediately obvious and discernible goals of the three lessons. However, a cursory consideration of the lessons suggest that the range of actual goals was rather wider than those that were immediately obvious or explicitly stated. Some additional *implicit* goals were not directly to do with the acquisition of *historical* knowledge or understanding (Coltham and Fines 1970). For example, the brainstorming activity and the picture exercise in the second lesson can be seen to have been a way of developing pupils' oracy (Howe 1992; Norman 1992). The writing exercise that followed the question and answer session in the first lesson can be seen to have been about giving pupils an opportunity to practise their writing (Sheeran and Barnes 1991; John 1994; Husbands 1996; Counsell 1997). Teachers are familiar with the notion of multiple goals: pupils read textbooks in history lessons to improve their understanding of history but also to enhance their reading skills. Information technology (IT) permits history teachers to access historical data in ways that would not otherwise be possible in the classroom, but this is also a way of enhancing pupils' IT capability. Where pupils work in groups around a computer in a history lesson the lesson may be 'about' history, IT skills and collaborative skills (Martin 1992). There is a further aspect of the multiplicity of goals. By focusing so far on the teacher, the whole class and the historical content, we may have neglected the ways in which teachers had *different* aspirations for different learners in the class (Postlethwaite 1993). Equally, we may have overlooked the fact that the teachers' concern was to devise a lesson in which particular pupils behaved appropriately. Some of the specific goals of a lesson may derive from the particular context in which the teacher finds himself or herself: from the time of day, the amount of space in the classroom or the lesson that went before. Finally, history teaching is also characterized by longer-term goals that may not be apparent in a single lesson: as an element in establishing open and critical thinkers in a democratic society (HMI 1985; Slater 1989, 1995; Visram 1994). The teachers in our three lessons were steering a course between overlapping and sometimes competing goals for the teaching of history.

Equally varied were the strategies for achieving the goals. The three teachers used a *range* of methods, including brainstorming, whole class interactive question and answer, pupils working alone, pupils working collaboratively, role-play, drama, teacher exposition and working with individuals (Waterhouse 1985). They used a chalkboard, textbooks, pictures and an overhead projector. Teachers chose what they believed to be the most appropriate strategy given the range of conditions and circumstances; not all of these conditions are explicit and not all relate either to the material or to the learners (Brown and McIntyre 1992).

Interaction in history classrooms

In all three of these lessons, the pupils were actively engaged in a variety of activities, and in each of the lessons at least some of these activities involved interaction between teachers and pupils or between pupils themselves. Pupils talked to each other in pairs, small groups and larger groups. They moved around the classroom. They shared ideas with the teacher and with each other. This may seem an obvious point but would not have been so, say, forty years ago; then, as far as we can tell from fairly limited evidence, it is far more likely that the pupils would have been the passive recipients of teacher exposition (Price 1968; Booth 1969; Sylvester 1994).

These ideas about classroom interaction led us into reflections on the language being used in these lessons (Edwards 1978; Levine 1981; Husbands 1996). Talk and writing were central features of the three lessons. They featured a wide range of language styles, genres, registers, and types. Language was spoken, written and read. It was used to explain ideas, to describe historical actions, to instruct and to organize pupils, to hypothesize about the past, to assess pupils' understandings, to encourage thought and to berate unacceptable behaviour (SCDC 1989; Gardiner 1992; John 1994). The list could go on. Language is such a taken-for-granted element of classroom history that it is easy to overlook its importance, and therefore both its potential and its difficulties (Giles and Neal 1983; ILEA 1983; McGill 1988; Morris 1992). It is critical to the teacher's ability to convey, in some accessible and meaningful way, the learning targets that have been selected for the lesson. It is critical to the way in which the teacher moves between the everyday language of pupils and the subject specific language of the subject (reform, total war, Whig, revolution) in order to support pupil learning. A sense of the relationship between language and learning is a key aspect of the range of questioning skills being used by teachers (Giles and Neal 1983). In the first lesson, the questions are organized in order to establish a relationship between content and what has gone on before, building on pupils' own ideas and probing their understandings before going on to introduce complex new material in linguistically accessible ways. In the second lesson, pupils' ideas about the content are used uncritically to establish a starting point and are subsequently tested against evidence. In the third lesson, pupils build an understanding of the past through their own language and movement around the classroom within a structure established by the teacher.

Pupil understandings and misunderstandings in history

There is a final set of issues that we want to consider from the evidence of our three lessons. In each of the three lessons, there were clear outcomes in terms of new understandings on the part of the pupils: they had developed hypotheses about the notion of total war, had acquired understandings of new historical concepts, had recognized that learning history could be enjoyable. The lessons produced, in a variety of ways, new *learning*. In none of the lessons were the outcomes necessarily, for all learners, clear-cut: the new understandings were at various levels of sophistication and depth, and in some cases, for some learners, the new understandings might have generated additional, or new misunderstandings (Ashby and Lee 1987; Booth 1987, 1993; Shemilt 1987; Dickinson *et al.* 1996). In the history classroom, teachers are concerned with both the modification of existing explanations through refinement (Pendry *et al.* 1997) and with the creation of new, restructured meanings, and with asking pupils to acquire information and to solve problems (Husbands 1996: ch. 6).

Developing history teaching

The goals of history teaching

This book is about teaching history in schools. The range of influences on the goals of history teaching in schools is particularly wide (Labbett 1979; Slater 1995). 'History' serves various purposes in society, and there are various different goals, sometimes contradictory and conflicting, for the study and teaching of the past (Ferro 1984; Skidelsky 1988; Husbands 1992; Husbands and Pendry 1992). History teachers, working as they do in publicly funded schools, operate within a framework of assumptions and expectations defined by others: by the state, by employers, by school managers and governors, by academic historians, by parents and by pupils themselves. These assumptions and expectations go some way towards pre-determining some of the goals of history teaching, and some of these pre-determined and externally imposed goals may not be open to direct question; others may be more so. Some teachers may agree with the externally imposed goals of history teaching, and others may not agree with all of them, but all have to find some way of defining their own relationship to the demands imposed by externally defined goals (Phillips 1993; Cooper and McIntyre 1996a). In England and Wales, history teachers working in the age range 5–14 are required to teach the national curriculum (DfEE 1994), which defines learning targets and content within an overall framework originally defined by the then Secretary of State for Education's (Kenneth Baker) directions to the History Working Group, which developed the national curriculum history framework. His instruction was that the teaching of history in schools, 'should help pupils to understand how a free and democratic society has developed over the centuries' (DES 1990:189). More recently, state agencies have looked to history to play a central role in the transmission of a 'common culture' or agreed inheritance to the next generation (McKiernan 1993; Tate 1995; Phillips 1997). All teachers in secondary schools work within a system that places a high premium on examination success. One goal for teachers is that they should help their pupils to gain the highest examination grades commensurate with their ability and effort.

Longer-term goals for the teaching of history may frequently remain implicit in the curricula and pedagogy of particular classrooms and schools rather than explicitly stated (Chancellor 1970). None the less, the tensions between them are reflected in the shorter term goals that frame lessons. Sequences of lessons may be about both the acquisition of knowledge and the critical scrutiny of evidence (Labbett 1979); curricula may encompass both the constitutional history of the nation and the experiences of the deprived and excluded, but the balance between them and the ways in which they are planned will reflect the ways in which teachers mediate between different goals and, echoing Lee, the ways in which they believe history has the capacity to 'change pupils' (Lee 1991). Unless history teachers are simply to be civil servants delivering an externally defined curriculum with externally defined goals in externally defined ways, a major task they face is clarifying and articulating what their goals are, what sorts of goals they are, whether they are purely historical or to do with more general educational goals, and the ways in which they relate to the wider goals of schools and the education system in the light of the multiple demands on the work of schools and teachers.

Learning history in classrooms

In exploring teachers' strategies we draw on a range of classroom- and teacher-based research, which over the past decade has illuminated the ways in which teachers and pupils think about and work together in classrooms to generate learning. In particular, we draw on the work of Paul Cooper and Donald McIntyre reported in *Effective Teaching and Learning* (Cooper and McIntyre 1996a; see also Cooper and McIntyre 1995), and on Anna Pendry's research on new teachers' planning and thinking (Pendry 1994, 1997). We take as our starting point Cooper's and McIntyre's suggestion that,

> the things teachers and pupils try to achieve in their classroom teaching and learning . . . offer very fruitful starting points for generating hypotheses about effective classroom teaching and learning. Only through knowing about teachers' and pupils' classroom practices and the thinking which underlies them, will it be possible to theorise . . . about the limitations of current practice . . . and . . . to plan intelligently for the development of classroom practice.
>
> (Cooper and McIntyre 1996a:3)

Based on a study of English and history teaching, Cooper and McIntyre identified 'some common aspects of teaching that were perceived to be effective' by teachers and their pupils (Cooper and McIntyre 1996a:158). They reject crude notions of 'good' or 'bad' practice. They argue that effective lesson strategies tend to be those based on a 'willingness to allow for different cognitive styles and ways of engaging in the learning process . . . through multiple exemplification, the use of different types of illustration and mode of presentation, and offering pupil a choice from a menu of possible ways of engaging' (1996a:158). Also important is the way that teachers 'take into account pupil circumstances and . . . modify/pace/ structure the learning task accordingly' (1996a:158). Finally, they note the importance of the classroom as a 'supportive social context designed by (the) teacher to help pupils feel accepted, cared for and valued' (1996a:158). Set in the context of these general conclusions about effective teaching, Cooper and McIntyre were able to construct a 'menu of methods' seen as effective aids to learning (Fig. 1.1).

Cooper's and McIntyre's analysis of classroom interaction draws on the work of the Russian psychologist Vygotsky (Vygotsky 1987). Vygotsky argued that the key to developing learners' capacities lay in their interaction with more experienced and expert adults. He

- Story telling (by the teacher)*
- Reading aloud (by the teacher/pupils)*
- Teacher mediation and modification of pupil verbal input to class discussions
- Oral explanation by the teacher, combined with discussion, question and answer sessions or use of chalkboard
- Chalkboard notes and diagrams as an *aide-mémoire*
- Use of pictures and other visual stimuli (for exploration/ information)*
- Use of explanatory models based on pupil ideas or generated by the teacher
- Structure for written work generated and presented by the teacher
- Group/pair work*
- Drama/role-play*
- Printed text
- Use of stimuli relating to pupils' 'pop' culture*

Figure 1.1 Activities and situations seen by teachers and pupils as aids to learning (Cooper and McIntyre 1996a:101). *Items cited by pupils as well as by teachers.

was attempting to provide a theory of intellectual development that acknowledged that children undergo quite profound changes in their understanding by engaging in joint activity and conversation with other people. The skill of the adult lay in his or her ability to mediate between the world about which they wished to teach, and what Vygotsky called the learner's 'zone of proximal development': 'the distance between the actual developmental level as determined by independent problem solving and the level of potential development as determined through problem solving under adult guidance or in collaboration with more capable peers' (1987:86). In the lessons we describe, the questioning, the brainstorming, the discussions and the opportunities for pupil interaction all provide ways in which these skilled teachers identify the relationship between the ideas they, as teachers have about the material, and their learners' perceptions, ideas and misconceptions (Bruner 1986; Vygotsky 1987). This 'transactional' relationship between teachers and learners is of particular significance when we consider the ways in which teachers use, address and correct pupils' misunderstandings and misconceptions about the subject matter. Over the past few years, we have become clearer about the role that pupils' misconceptions play in learning. Guy Claxton (1993) suggests that one way of thinking about learning is to consider the ideas pupils themselves bring into lessons as 'mini theories': 'conceptual maps which give learners ways of explaining aspects of the world' (1993:46). Mini theories are fragmentary and often contradictory. On the mini theory view, there are a number of main types of learning. One involves modification of existing modules (of explanation), and another involves the creation of a new, purpose-built mini theory to deal with a new domain of experience. [A third possibility] is 'restructuring the existing gut/lay mini theory so that a full understanding and resolution of the conflict results' (Claxton 1993:49).

Derek Edwards and Neil Mercer have drawn on exceptionally detailed classroom research to explore the ways in which 'common knowledge' or shared understandings emerge as a result of communicative interaction between teachers and pupils (Edwards and Mercer 1992). They see this as neither a straightforward nor unproblematic exercise: the negotiation of shared meanings invariably involves a balance between presenting and sharing knowledge, between building understandings and encountering and resolving misunderstandings. It calls for, and typically is served by, according to the Edwards and Mercer evidence, considerable skill on the part of teachers. Chris Husbands's *What is History Teaching?* (Husbands 1996) identifies a variety of language demands in learning history. There is a specialist vocabulary of the past ('beadle', 'reeve', 'villein'), a further vocabulary of words that had different meanings in the past to those that they have now (for example, 'revolution') and a further set of historical labels that are used to convey complex, and often larger ideas (perhaps most obviously class, or period labels like Tudors or Georgians). There is a vocabulary of historical time which pupils need to learn ('era', 'century', 'decade'), and a language of historical analysis – the language of causation and consequence, for example. Finally, there is a language of historical debate; the way in which some events and individuals are described – as freedom fighter or guerrilla, hero or villain – is also a way of setting them into a framework of values. For these reasons, Husbands argued that language in the history classroom is best seen as an 'interpretive system'; a way of exploring meanings and probing assumptions (Husbands 1996:30–8, 41). It is precisely the tentative, often discursive and fragmentary nature of language that makes it a vehicle for interpretive use. Words, as Gardiner puts it, can be 'surprisingly disciplined squads' for attacking complex and unfamiliar material (Gardiner 1992:197). In the classroom, Husbands argues for an approach to the use of language that emphasizes a concern for the way in which words shape thinking and talking about the past, as a way of exploring ideas and for contexts in which teachers support pupils' exploration and understanding of the past through a variety of structured contexts for talk, reading and writing. He sets out a process for classroom writing, examining, rather in the way our three teachers did, different sorts of writing for different classroom purposes (the initial thought, the collection of data, the processing of ideas and the drafting and production of written reports) (Husbands 1996:41, 115).

This book is about the professional learning of history teachers as they prepare to enter the profession, in their early years as history teachers and as they develop their expertise. It emphasizes the complexity of history teaching, of understanding teacher and pupil perspectives and the need to ground professional development in the realities of classroom interaction. It draws on a range of research based evidence in order to inform the development of practice. It does not propose that the task of becoming or developing as a history teacher is either simple or straightforward, and, indeed, it is founded on a respect for the professional skills and knowledge of practitioners. What it does propose is that if we use such expertise as the basis for professional learning then we have the opportunity to enhance both the initial preparation of history teachers and their continuing development. It has a simple structure. Part 1 focuses on learning to teach and ways of supporting and directing this learning. It examines the ways in which teachers' own initial ideas about their work and the discipline of history are powerful influences on the way they teach, and identifies strategies and procedures for developing the quality of beginning teachers' classroom practice. Part 2 focuses on newly qualified teachers and considers ways in which teacher development in the early years of a career can be enhanced through reflection on the classroom and the discipline. Part 3 explores the possibilities for professional learning by members of a history department, setting the aspirations of individuals in the context of concern to enhance the quality of pupil learning in history. It concludes by outlining a broad rationale for the teaching and learning of history in schools in a culturally diverse, open society.

Part One

INITIAL TEACHER EDUCATION

Anna Pendry and Chris Husbands

2

LEARNING TO TEACH HISTORY

The goals of history teacher education

All those involved in teacher education – students, mentors, tutors, examiners, government agencies – typically share a simple goal: they want to design programmes of teacher education that help, as far as possible, to produce good new teachers. Put like this, the goals of teacher education seem simplistic in the extreme; so obvious, perhaps, as to be scarcely worth a second thought. But the consensus, and the simplicity, are deceptive. 'Good teaching', and the 'production' of good teachers, is complex and difficult. 'Good teachers' are those who can motivate, enthuse and stimulate youngsters' learning through their command of their subject, their commitment to young people and their abilities to deploy a variety of resources and teaching and learning strategies; they are those who can control classes of adolescents and deliver the requirements of the national curriculum. They are those who can offer structured learning support to learners for whom learning is difficult, and stimulate and extend the thinking of the exceptionally able. They are those who can think imaginatively and creatively about their subject and develop new approaches to teaching it that will ensure that schools are innovative, successful institutions. They are those who will, after developing their class-room skills, go on to take a leadership role on academic or pastoral aspects of schools' work. When Her Majesty's Inspectorate of schools (HMI) set out to describe the work of good teachers in the mid 1980s, they found it difficult to crystallize their ideas: 'It is given to few teachers to possess all the good qualities mentioned, and many will vary in style and personality without necessarily being better or worse for their differences' (HMI 1985:13). The demands placed on teacher education, then, are more complex, and possibly contradictory than initially appeared to be the case. There are difficult balances to be struck between consolidating new teachers' subject knowledge in relation to the national curriculum and developing their range of pedagogic strategies; between helping them to develop approaches to teaching history to pupils with learning difficulties and helping them teach the very able. In a crowded curriculum, difficult choices have to be made, and the way they are made will often reflect the priorities that are given by different stakeholders to different goals for initial teacher education (ITE).

In England, at least, the State now has a direct and close involvement in the determination of the goals and nature of ITE in schools. The national standards for newly qualified teachers (NQTs) (DfEE 1997a) set out in considerable detail the expectations that the State has of newly qualified teachers under four broad headings: subject knowledge and understanding; planning, teaching and classroom management; assessment, monitoring and accountability; and 'other professional requirements'. The task of initial teacher education is to ensure that these standards are met. Some of them are particularly detailed: 'structuring information well, including outlining content and aims, signalling transitions and summarising key points as the lesson progresses' (DfEE 1997a:9, B2k (iii)). More specifically, the Department for Education and Employment (DfEE) has expressed a narrow set of goals for initial teacher training (ITT): 'The National Curriculum has . . . made explicit that which has to be taught. It is, however, one thing to understand what is required for the National Curriculum and another to be able to teach the subject and respond to the needs and abilities of one's pupils' (Millet 1996:4). The involvement of the State in setting the goals of ITE is relatively recent, and has changed markedly over its short history (Alexander 1984; Wilkin 1996; Brooks and Sikes 1997). In 1984, the government took powers to prescribe requirements for courses of ITE (DES 1984). In 1992, it took powers to define, in rather broad terms, the expected entry competencies of newly qualified teachers (DfE 1992). In 1994, the government established the Teacher Training Agency (TTA), a departmental body of the DfEE charged with funding initial and continuing teacher education and with managing teacher supply (Mahoney and Hextall 1997).

The national standards (DfEE 1997a) are the product of the work of the TTA, and represent a particular expression of current political goals for ITT. Clearly, any programme of teacher education must be informed about this particular statement of goals and must link its own goals demonstrably to this statutory requirement. Much within the list of competencies is uncontroversial as a requirement for ITE. None the less, the national standards make some assumptions about the goals of teacher education that are worth exploring. The standards place considerable emphasis on the acquisition of high levels of subject knowledge, defined narrowly in terms of the national curriculum (DfEE 1997a: A1(ii)) and the demands of subject examination syllabuses (DfEE 1997a: A1(iv)), rather than, for example, on the notion of a wider understanding of different approaches to and forms of the discipline. For example, the standards do not require newly qualified history teachers to be well informed about recent developments in historiography. They emphasize formal, interactive teaching skills (DfEE 1997a: B2k), but say relatively little about areas of classroom practice such as helping pupils to undertake investigative activity. All this suggests that the State's requirements for teacher education provide at best a partial account of the goals of teacher education: choices still have to be made (Stronach *et al.* 1996).

Different courses of teacher education themselves define individual aims for teacher education (Benton 1990; McIntyre 1990; Williams 1994). An important national survey of ITE in the early 1990s found that most courses were, in some way, based around the idea of developing students as 'reflective practitioners' (Schön 1983, 1987; Calderhead 1989; Barrett *et al.* 1993). By this, ITE institutions appeared to mean that they were setting out to provide courses that enabled students not only to teach effectively as classroom practitioners, but also to reflect critically on their work both in the context of their own classroom, and in the context of the school curriculum. In terms of history, such goals would indicate aspirations not only to equip students with knowledge and understanding of the national curriculum in order to teach it, but also to encourage them to consider why it takes the form it does and to be professionally critical of the national curriculum (Pendry 1990). Students would be expected to learn how to set, assess and record GCSE and A-level coursework, but also to be aware of the limitations of such assessment methods. Perhaps most important, such courses would attempt to ensure that students not only taught effective lessons, but could be self-critical about the content chosen and the methods adopted. There may be fewer contradictions between such approaches and the *formal* national requirements than this brief sketch suggests (Gilroy 1992): where the government is concerned with outcomes, these aspirations are concerned with processes and patterns of courses. None the less, there is clearly tension between the conception of the history teacher as classroom technician, which underpins the TTA model, and the notion of the teacher as autonomous professional, which is implied in the Modes of Teacher Education Project (MOTE) survey. Although McIntyre and Cooper have rightly and succinctly warned against the assumption that reflective practice is necessarily good practice (Cooper and McIntyre 1996a:5), the notions that have underpinned course development and goal setting in the last few years seem to provide some useful pointers to ways of developing teacher education.

Although these national and course-level expressions of goals are important, ITE increasingly, and rightly, rests in the hands of school-based mentors. So far, we appear to know relatively little about the way school-based mentors in history choose and set goals for their student teachers' learning (Booth 1993). Mentors face tensions in their daily practice with student teachers: for them, the students' success is likely to depend in some large measure on the ability to learn about, and acclimatize to, the institutional expectations of the individual school (Feiman-Nemser *et al.* 1993). Research in other subject areas suggests, perhaps not surprisingly, that there is an enormous range from those who take a highly mechanistic view to those who share notions of reflective practice in its broadest sense (Abbott *et al.* 1995; Allsop and Benson 1997; Brooks and Sikes 1997). There is some evidence that mentors select goals and learning targets fairly ruthlessly; in research on assessment – to which goals relate fairly closely – it has been suggested that 'practitioners seemed to find it difficult in practice to assess trainees against more than about six significant criteria . . . In practice we found that teacher educators tended to reduce the lists of competencies specified by the Department for Education to not more than six broad categories' (Bridges *et al.* cited in Brooks and Sikes 1997:129). In the absence of more detailed empirical research, we hypothesize that effective mentors will make choices about goals for their work with student teachers that rest on a balance between national requirements, course frameworks, school culture and what they see as the needs, and strengths, of the student teachers themselves.

So far, we have not considered the student teachers' perspective on the goals of ITE, but they are significant. Student teachers in history are, typically, highly educated adults, who have already secured a first degree, and, statistics suggest in about 30 per cent of cases, have acquired extensive work experience *before* deciding to enter teaching (Graduate Teacher Training Registry 1996). At one level, they share the generic, and uncontroversial goal of all the other stakeholders in teacher education: they want to become good history teachers. However, each student is an individual and as such will have a distinctive personality, particular skills, interests and concerns. Consider, for example, the following three students.

- Wendy left school at 16 and by the age of 20 was married with three children. Her marriage broke up in her early twenties. When her youngest daughter entered secondary schooling, she embarked on a higher education Access course at her local further education (FE) college and completed a degree in history and politics at her local university. She decided to become a teacher through her interest in, and work with, her daughters as they made their way through secondary schooling – she couldn't quite believe that she had decided to do so, when she remembered how badly she had behaved at school!
- Mark, whose father had been an eminent classics academic was educated at a boys' public school and took a first class honours degree in history and philosophy. He was fascinated by the history of ideas, and went on to do an MA in Medieval History, writing a Master's thesis on medieval philosophy. He'd hoped to secure funding for a PhD but failed to do so. Unwilling to abandon the academic subject he found so fascinating, he decided to become a teacher.
- Sean graduated with a history degree, and had been sabbatical vice-president of the Students' Union for a year as an undergraduate. After graduating he worked in a variety of jobs for five years: he was a pizza delivery driver, a gardener, a painter and decorator and joined a road protest for six months, before ending up on an archaeological dig. He found that he enjoyed talking about the dig to school parties brought to the site and decided to become a teacher.

Each of these students, like all others, bring with them strong ideas about the nature and value of history and of schooling (Wilson and Wineburg 1988; Bird *et al.* 1993). For some students history is a powerful and fascinating story about the past; a story worth knowing about 'for its own sake', which is intrinsically interesting. Mark, for example, had always loved history. Others are more concerned with the conceptual nature of the subject and for them its study may be seen as of value in understanding the present: understanding why things happen and why people act as they do is a liberating force. Wendy had drifted into history through her daughters' schoolwork, and found her university work on women's history a source of understanding about her own life and experiences. Yet others may simply have enjoyed history themselves but are most concerned that through its study one can learn a range of transferable skills of use in, for example, analysing given information, criticizing media accounts and constructing persuasive arguments. For Sean, history was a down-to-earth business about the daily lives of people in the past.

Most, if not all, history graduates begin their professional training with some of these ideas and such ideas will have an enduring influence on the sort of history they think is worth learning and the sorts of justifications they have for their subject in school. They may even already be linked in their minds to the sorts of things they want to do and achieve in history classrooms. Wendy had found history intolerably dull at school and was determined that her lessons would be 'different'; Mark had enjoyed school history and wanted his lessons to be as 'good' as the ones he had been taught; Sean believed that good history was only possible if he could take his pupils outside the classroom to historic sites.

Students are equally likely to begin with powerful, if sometimes naive, ideas about what learning *is*, about what learning history involves and about the teacher's role in relation to these ideas. They have fairly clear ideas about what is, and what is not, an effective teacher, perhaps related to their own positive and negative experiences as pupils and consequently about the sort of teacher they do or do not want to be (Calderhead and Robson 1991). It is highly likely that they will begin their professional training with pronounced ideas about the purpose of education in general and how they, as teachers, will contribute to this. Wendy and Sean were clear about the ways they wanted to realize certain values through their teaching of history, Mark's ideas, although less clearly expressed, were none the less distinctive. Finally, it is likely that they will also come with ideas both about what they need to learn for their existing ideas to be turned into realities for them, and how they will learn these things (Pendry 1994).

Although it may be tempting to see student teachers as 'blank pages', it is hardly surprising that the years they have spent in school as pupils and as students in higher education, their experiences as sisters, brothers and parents and the years of reading newspapers and watching television will have resulted in the formulation of a wide range of beliefs about history, teaching and learning (Lortie 1975). Students have made a committed and thoughtful decision to enter teaching so mentors and tutors should not be surprised if such a commitment is based upon firm beliefs. These beliefs generally prove to be enduring; they will have been developed over many years and many experiences, and although, for many, initial training proves to be a fairly extraordinary experience, it is none the less relatively brief. Research study after research study has shown the extent and significance of the ideas that beginner teachers bring with them, and how these ideas are one of the most important determinants of what they take from their programme of teacher education. It seems that new teachers' own ideas act as a filter or lens through which all that they experience in their training must pass. Whilst these ideas are stable, this does not mean that they are inflexible; they can change and develop and thus it is important for tutors and mentors to engage with them. Although most researchers have been dismissive or critical of students' initial ideas (McDiarmid *et al.* 1989; Kagan 1992; Rovegno 1992), more recent work suggests that they are not necessarily unhelpful (Guillame and Rudney 1993; Bullough with Stokes 1994; Pendry 1994). Although it may be that some view learning in history as simply the accumulation of more knowledge, believe that the role of the teacher is primarily to tell pupils about what happened and think that all learners will be like them – love history, be successful, go on to university – others may view learning much more as a process of developing understandings for oneself, will see the role of the teacher as involved in finding ways for pupils, as individuals, to achieve this and will understand and accept that pupils have a wide range of capabilities and legitimate aspirations.

It is unhelpful both to accept uncritically the ideas of new trainees or simply to ignore them as wrong or misleading. In the first case, mentors and tutors fail to enable the students to scrutinize for themselves their ideas and see if, in the context of school history teaching, about which they are now becoming knowledgeable, these ideas are sustainable. If they are, they will be all the more powerful and secure as ideas to help provide direction and purpose for the beginner. In the second case, what is most likely to happen is that the ideas will be submerged and go underground; tenaciously retained but infrequently articulated. It is highly unlikely that student teachers will simply change their ideas; they are most likely to say little about them, and emerge from teacher education programmes relatively unscathed and untouched (Zeichner and Liston 1987; Zeichner 1993). Since these ideas are likely to help explain much of what the student teacher does and does not do and learn during training, it is important for mentors and tutors to find out what they are. They can be discovered through discussion with students, but also, for example, by listening to their commentaries on other teachers' teaching, observing their reactions to feedback on their own teaching and hearing their views of curriculum or learning innovations. Having found out what they are, mentors and tutors need to tread a delicate balance between legitimizing and challenging students' ideas (Elliott and Calderhead 1993). Effective mentoring will help student teachers to explore their grounds for holding such views and their implications: working with existing ideas rather than against them. Such an approach may, of course, include helping students to see that certain ideas, although reasonable from a certain perspective, are in practice both unhelpful and untenable. It may also involve accepting that in many cases there are valid, different points of view – about the purposes for learning history, about what certain pupils are capable of achieving in history, about the most appropriate strategy to use – and that these differences cannot be easily resolved. The student may finish the course with views about teaching history that differ in fundamental respects to those held by the mentor or tutor, and these are entirely reasonable views to hold.

Each of these groups of stakeholders have different expectations of, and goals for, teacher education. In some cases the goals overlap; in other cases they are contradictory. In all cases, the way in which goals are selected depends on preconceptions and context as much as on national or statutory frameworks. We do not propose now to attempt to reconcile the difference between different goals and expectations, or to accept some and reject others; rather, we want to provide a framework in which teachers, mentors and students can articulate their own goals, aware of, but not constrained by, the national standards and the statutory framework. We begin with the argument sketched in Chapter 1: a commitment to history teaching that is complex, concerned with a wide range of different sorts of goals, with interaction between teachers and learners and with the development of new historical understandings. We argued there that all history teachers are fundamentally concerned with some key questions, which themselves help new teachers and their mentors to consider their work and their goals:

- What do I want to achieve?
- How do I want to achieve that?
- How will I know if I've achieved that?
- What might have prevented me from achieving it?

What do I want to achieve?

Student teachers *do* need to learn about the prescribed goals of the National Curriculum, GCSE, A level and other externally defined syllabuses. They *do* need to learn about the particular ways these have been interpreted by both the schools in which they are actually working and others. They *do* need to learn about selecting and setting appropriate goals for pupils of different ages, given what we know about children's learning in history. They *do* need to learn about the ways in which they might adjust their goals to take account of the diverse characteristics of the pupils with whom they will be working. Beyond this, they need to consider their own versions of the nature of history and what it is that they think is important about history and that makes it worth learning: history, like others, is a contested subject (Fines 1987; Sanders 1994:29; Davies 1996). They need to take into account what their own skills make it possible for them to achieve in their lessons and which of their goals may need to wait until they are more skilful practitioners. They need to learn about the relationships between the goals they may have for an individual lesson and for a series of lessons (Ofsted 1997b). They need support to learn how to make these decisions about goals, and how to make these decisions in ways that will lead them to have goals that are sufficiently focused to be of real value to them and to the learners who they will be teaching.

These issues outline an agenda for beginner teachers, but they will also need to be focused on the planning of particular lessons and learning experiences (MacLennan 1987; John 1993; Ofsted 1997b). Beginners will have aspirations for their lessons from the outset, but these are likely to be expressed in broad and very general terms at first, and in so far as they are specific it will be historical content that is specified – to consider the causes of the French Revolution or to look at the outbreak of the First World War or the Black Death. They will need a great deal of help in making these more specific and in limiting them; in relating historical content to the more classroom-specific questions of defining the targets of pupil learning within particular areas of content. Their initial goals are likely to be much more concerned with themselves than with the pupils (for them to 'cover —'), and in so far as they are concerned with pupils, they are likely to be primarily concerned with the need to occupy pupils. They will need support to move gradually away from a preoccupation with teaching and classroom management to a concern for pupil learning. For example, they might, quite legitimately want to teach pupils about the causes of the English Civil War, but will need considerable help in turning this into a set of goals for a lesson that enable them to select appropriate learning activities and to evaluate the success of their work in the classroom. Furthermore, initially, our experience and acquaintance with research evidence suggests that beginners are unlikely to be able to think sensibly about more than one lesson at a time (Pendry 1994). If they can begin to express goals for those in ways that take account of the learners as well as the history and the teacher then they will be doing well; setting goals for a series of lessons can only come much later. This is both a signpost and a warning to them and their mentors about what might be realistic expectations early in a placement. Finally, it is likely that it will only be in the light of students' developing knowledge of pupils, classrooms and learning, and of their developing expertise as competent teachers, that they will be able to make real sense of goals prescribed by others, such as the national curriculum requirements, and articulate their own goals in a way that is of practical value to them.

As they become competent and concerned with pupil learning, they will be ready to ask questions about the value of their goals: how do I know if it was worth achieving? Although overemphasis on this sort of question early on is more likely than not to discourage beginner teachers, students do need to learn both the relevance of the question and the variety of responses that there may be to it. It may be that the principal aim of a given activity, such as copying text from the board, is that it keeps the pupils quiet. If they have been repeatedly noisy and disruptive in previous lessons then this may constitute a worthwhile 'success' in the short term, but the attribution of value or worth needs to recognize that it is *this* that has been achieved and not something else. Low-level activities that serve the purpose of management and control are not *in themselves* valid learning activities, so that leading students to believe such activities to be worth while in terms of immediate learning gains would be dishonest, or at least self-deluding on the part of the teacher. A wide range of criteria might be applied in thinking about the worth of what has been achieved, criteria that range from feasibility and practicality to association with the nature of history or one's goals as a teacher. It is highly unlikely that all the criteria in terms of which one might judge one's teaching will be satisfied all the time. It is, however, important to continue to ask the question, employing the full range of criteria, and to examine which, if any, are repeatedly omitted.

How do I want to achieve that?

Of primary concern for beginning history teachers are the activities that will go on in their lesson; what they will do and what the pupils will do. For beginner teachers, activity is seen as the way to counteract indiscipline. Lesson plans are therefore something like scripts, and in order to compile a script, beginners need to develop a repertoire of all the possible valid activities for history lessons:

involving reading, writing, watching, listening and talking; for individuals, for pairs, for small groups and for whole classes. They need to learn about these in practice; what needs to be done to initiate, manage and conclude them in the classroom; what might be achieved or learned through them; and how different strategies relate to the goals that they have for their lessons. They need the opportunity to try these out for themselves, initially in relatively protected environments (Burn 1992, 1997). They need to learn about how they can choose from all the options available to them and what, in any given set of circumstances, will represent an appropriate choice.

The range of ideas that beginners have initially is likely to be strongly influenced by their own educational experience. They need lots of opportunities to find out about a wider range of possibilities, whatever their own experiences have been. Beginners also need help in translating the *idea* of an activity into practice; they are often unaware of all that the teacher has to do in order to make an activity happen in the classroom. Students need teachers to make this explicit to them, both through discussing teaching observed by the student and through discussing their own plans. Of course, most classroom activities require multiple skills of teachers. For example, a question and answer session demands skills in projecting voice (Comyns 1996), choosing appropriate language (Husbands 1996), managing pupils' responses (Wragg and Brown 1993), controlling pupils' attention (Robertson 1981) and so on. Recent work has emphasized particularly the extent to which language plays a crucial role in the construction of understandings in history (Husbands 1996: ch. 3).

A further characteristic of history is the extent to which it deals with relatively abstract concepts and abstract knowledge (Edwards 1978; Shemilt 1980). Beginners need the opportunity to *learn* the range of skills involved here. It makes sense to start with relatively simple activities and language, and concepts that are less demanding but that can increasingly be combined to make more complex teaching and learning feasible. The grounds on which beginners choose activities, like their choice of goals, is likely to be strongly influenced initially by what they feel confident in achieving and by what is likely to keep pupils 'safely' occupied. It will only be as they develop in skill and confidence that they will be able to make and carry through choices that are informed by a wide range of considerations.

How will I know if I've achieved that?

Learning how to evaluate teaching and learning and how to take account of such evaluation is an important goal for beginners, although the question as expressed may not be high on their list of priorities. Their most immediate concern is likely to be 'if it went alright'; i.e. did they succeed in doing their bit? did the pupils do what they were asked to do? As evaluation questions these are entirely reasonable and sensible, and it is unlikely that anything else will have been achieved if one of these conditions has not been met. Beginners need to learn how to evaluate their own teaching and then the pupils' learning in more sophisticated terms. They need to learn about what the criteria for evaluation might be, and the implications of different criteria: will they be their goals for their own learning; their goals for the pupils' historical learning; their goals for the pupils' behaviour; or their goals for individual pupils? They need to learn about what sorts of evidence they can call on to see if the criteria have been met, including: their own perceptions of what happened; the feedback that an observer can offer; the pupils' work; or conversations with pupils. They need to learn about how they can take account of what they have discovered from such evaluation.

Although any really valuable evaluation of teaching must take account of learning, initially beginners should not be expected to be able to think very clearly about that learning. They should be encouraged to think, from a very early stage, about the effects of their actions (e.g. evaluating their instructions in terms of whether or not pupils know what to do, and an explanation in terms of its clarity to pupils), but it will take time before they can do this in terms of anything other than a fairly superficial idea of pupils' learning. As they progress, it is important to encourage them to think in these terms, and not be satisfied by evaluation that does not take account of an honest appraisal of learning outcomes. We should anticipate that evaluation may happen more in the planning for the next lesson than in the aftermath of the last; it seems likely that it is the moment when evaluation matters in a real sense. Many beginners will need considerable help in arriving at balanced evaluations; for many, everything is either 'fine' or 'terrible'. They may need support in 'seeing' and accepting that the pupils were actually very confused or, alternatively, that just because three pupils did no work at all then it may not be the case that the lesson achieved nothing for most of the pupils.

What might have prevented me from achieving it?

In many ways this is just one dimension of the evaluation questions that beginners need to ask of themselves, but for all teachers it is important that they learn to put their own actions into a broader context. Evaluation and a recognition of what was not achieved needs to be considered not just in terms of what the individual failed to do or did badly, but also in terms of the influence of other factors. Pupils bring into school with them a range of understandings, misunderstandings and prejudices about the past. For example, they may find it very hard to grasp the significance of religion in the history of medicine if they come from a secular background. It may be that the pupils failed to understand the significance of the Chartist movement because the teacher did not explain it sufficiently or design activities that adequately enabled the pupils to explore the motives of those leading the movement. Such a lack of understanding might also be attributed to the fact that teachers can realistically only spend a limited number of lessons on this topic if all the other requirements of the syllabus are to be met, and as a result it is likely that pupils' understanding can only be partial. It may be that the rather uneven progression of some pupils in the year following transfer from primary schools is because the teacher has failed to plan adequately for such progression, but it may also be attributable to the fact that the secondary school has 14 feeder schools with diverse ways of teaching history. It may be that many lessons are a struggle in terms of the management of the pupils because the teacher has failed to master basic management strategies, but it could be due to an inadequate school policy on rewards and sanctions and little support from senior management over such concerns. Thus, goals may not be achieved for reasons that are attributable to an individual teacher, and in their control, but it may be that the reason lies in what learners bring to their lesson, in the school as a whole, in the relations between schools or in the more general practices of the educational system. Like other teachers, beginners need to learn about these possibilities and to view teaching as, in part, the art of the possible.

This question also raises a distinctive issue for some beginners. It is common for some, especially if they are having problems, to deflect most, if not all, blame for classroom failure away from themselves and their own teaching, and to blame either the pupils or the context in which they find themselves (Lacey 1977). Thus, it is because the pupils didn't listen or didn't make an effort that they didn't complete the task, or group work isn't possible because the pupils in this school are badly behaved. Providing opportunities for beginner teachers to understand pupil perspectives and expectations (Harris and Rudduck 1993; Rudduck *et al.* 1996), and to become very much part of the school may help to alleviate this strategy for coping with failure.

The processes of learning to teach history

Our initial statement of an apparently straightforward, common-sensical goal for teacher education – to become a good teacher – has now developed into a complex series of questions that need to underpin dialogue about history teaching among tutors, mentors and students. We have suggested that decisions need to be made about goals for teacher education and that making these decisions depends on being aware of statutory and course requirements as well as on school contexts and individual student teachers' starting points. Although student teachers are individuals, and as a result the process of learning to teach is relatively idiosyncratic, there are none the less certain generalizations that support goal setting at different stages of learning to teach. Over the last decade, a series of research studies and programmes have attempted to define 'phases' or 'stages' in the process of learning to teach. For example, as Furlong and Maynard (1995) identify, a particularly influential study was that of Fuller and Brown (1975), who identified three stages: survival; mastery; and then either routinization and resistance to change or concern with their impact on pupils. Calderhead (1987) has similarly suggested three phases in learning to teach, labelling them 'fitting in', 'passing the test' and 'exploring'. Much more recently, Furlong and Maynard themselves (1995) have identified five broad stages. An 'early idealism' is followed by a phase of concern for 'personal survival' and being seen as a teacher. The third stage is 'dealing with difficulties', essentially through the mimicry of experienced teachers. As teaching, from their teacher centred perspective, becomes manageable, students enter the fourth stage, 'hitting a plateau', and the final stage, if they go this far, is 'moving on'.

Furlong and Maynard emphasize that, although they were able to identify such stages, they were neither simple nor linear and were highly dependent on a unique interaction between an individual student, their teacher education programme and school context. Thus they describe each student's learning as 'complex, erratic and in one sense unique to them as an individual' (Furlong and Maynard 1995:70), a finding echoed by Pendry in her study of beginning history teachers' lesson planning. She concluded that 'there was no evidence in this study of common stages of development for the student teachers – a finding which seems consistent with the evidence of the idiosyncrasies of their learning and the influence of their differing personal preconceptions' (1994:205). However, her study was concerned with planning, not classroom teaching, and it may be that it is primarily in the context of actual teaching that such stages can be discerned. None the less Pendry and Furlong and Maynard support the contention that 'student teachers in this study did not so much think about different things as they grew; they thought about things differently' (Guillame and Rudney 1993:79).

Models of learning to teach

Fuller and Brown (1975)

Survival → Mastery ⤱ Routinization
                 ⤲ Concern with impact on pupils

Calderhead (1987)

Fitting in → Passing the test → Exploring

Furlong and Maynard (1995)

                     Dealing
Idealism → Survival →   with   → Plateau → Moving on
                  difficulties

These qualifications are useful warnings against an over-schematic approach to 'phases' in learning to teach; 'becoming a teacher is inevitably an idiosyncratic process' (Bullough 1992:251). However, although there are no discrete linear phases in the process of learning to teach, there do appear to be some common features (Kagan 1992; Dunkin 1996). An initial preoccupation with self as a teacher is very common among beginners, and a concern for pupils' learning comes much later. In the early stages of learning to be a teacher, concerns about classroom management and control are often dominant. Fitting in and 'passing' are very real preoccupations for student teachers, and until students are assured that they are 'passing' in some way they are highly unlikely to take risks in their teaching. Finally, there is likely to be a large gap between what student teachers can manage to think about to do with their teaching and what they can actually attend to in the classroom itself, and there are likely to be large differences in the degrees of fluency in all that they do in the classroom; they will progress at different rates in relation to different aspects of teaching. It follows that mentors need to provide repeated opportunities for student teachers to learn about issues of management and control and to understand how these are related to issues of teaching and learning. They also need to give a variety of examples of ways in which students can plan and carry out activities that will minimize unnecessary management problems, to help students to learn about ways of asserting themselves, and to encourage

students to concentrate on their own use of language in the classroom when giving instructions and explanations and questioning. If
mentors or tutors ignore student concerns then it is they who will
be ignored: students' initial concerns will not be dissipated until
they have had adequate opportunities to learn the appropriate skills
and knowledge to overcome them. The moment they begin to
achieve this is when mentors and tutors should alert students to the
challenge of really bringing about learning in history classrooms.

Professional growth then, like teaching itself, is complex and
multidimensional; it involves changes in knowledge, beliefs and
skills (Calderhead 1988). It involves different forms of learning; students need to learn both *to* teach and *about* teaching. It occurs in a
range of contexts and it requires both support and challenge (Elliott
and Calderhead 1993). Not surprisingly, given all this, student teachers
need opportunities to learn in a wide range of ways: by teaching
themselves and receiving feedback on that teaching; by observing
others teaching and discussing their teaching; by discussing their
ideas and the ideas of others with other students, with teachers, with
their tutors and with pupils; and by reading and listening. Some of
these ways of learning will be familiar to student teachers but others
will be new, and some that are familiar – like learning from reading – will have a new function now: much more concerned with
formulating plans for action rather than just collecting information.
Depending on their existing ideas about what they have to learn
and how they will learn those things, students may need to be
persuaded of the merits of some of these ways of learning. Students
need help to see that certain ways of learning are more appropriate
for particular targets; if they want to really understand why an
experienced history teacher explained a topic in a particular way
they will need to ask that teacher, not just make their own infer-
ences from observation (Hagger 1997).

The concern here is with student history teachers' learning in the
context of school, although clearly they will be learning in a wide
range of contexts: formally in a university or college; informally at
home; on their own; with friends; and so on. That much of student teacher learning is to take place in school presents distinctive
challenges. It might seem that a school is the ideal place. After all,
schools are *for* learning, and they are the locations in which teaching
takes place. However, on the whole, schools are not places where
the main function of adults is to learn. They are predominantly places
in which children learn and are environments where to be a learner
means to be a child or adolescent, whereas being an adult means
being a teacher or member of the support staff. This places student

teachers in a difficult position. On the one hand they want to 'fit in', which probably means 'being a teacher', and on the other hand this is precisely the role they need to 'learn'. The desire to fit in and be like a real teacher can lead student teachers to become so socialized into the school that they can no longer adopt a critical, learning perspective on what they are doing (Constable and Norton 1994). It becomes a matter of teaching in ways that are acceptable to this institution, rather than a process of *learning about teaching*.

Edwards and Collison (1996), in their study of primary student teachers, describe the relationship between student teachers and their mentors as a guest host relationship; student teachers bringing gifts of ideas for lessons that are gratefully received by their hosts, provided that they can be implemented in ways that do not disturb the status quo. Professional learning depends rather more on student teachers becoming part of the school community. This in itself can also help their learning, and at the same time ensure that they have many opportunities to learn in and from that environment.

The evidence suggests that four strategies may help here. The first is an explicit recognition that the issue is a difficult one that creates potential tensions for all parties, and that classrooms are only likely to be fertile grounds for professional learning if certain steps are taken by mentors and students (McIntyre 1994). Secondly, 'legitimate peripheral participation' is a useful concept. It involves helping student teachers, and all those working with them, including the pupils, to recognize that being part of classrooms and operating in limited ways within them is a reasonable activity for adults to undertake (Lave, cited in Edwards and Collison 1996:26). A third way of responding to this challenge is to try to ensure that all that student teachers are doing is regarded as an opportunity for them to learn; explicitly identified as such and discussed in terms of that learning (Hagger *et al.* 1995). Finally, a whole school commitment to initial teacher education is critical. It may assist staff and pupils, as well as the student teacher, to see the student's engagement in the school as far more than a 'teaching practice' when they borrow classes from experienced staff and do their best to act like them (Shaw 1992; Wynn 1994).

Learning to teach history is far from straightforward, and is frequently challenging for students and for those working alongside them. We have emphasized the ways in which this learning nests within a context defined by statutory obligations, professional expectations and, importantly, the assumptions and presuppositions of beginning teachers. Effective learning by student history teachers depends on the stakeholders in their professional development explicitly recognizing the importance of these ideas, and designing learning strategies that reflect both these starting points and the insights we now have from research into the process of learning to teach. In Chapter 3, we move to an explicit consideration of practical strategies to support such learning.

3

MENTORING STUDENT TEACHERS

The single most important person in the life of a student teacher is the mentor. Student teachers repeatedly attest to this, and their highest praise and deepest disappointments are reserved for their mentors. At its best, effective mentoring can make students' experiences wholly positive; at its worst it can severely limit a students' learning. Just as pupils deserve good teachers, so student teachers deserve good mentors (Booth 1993; Rothwell *et al.* 1994). By mentor we mean the history subject specialist who takes responsibility for the student teacher's learning in school. Mentors will work closely with students and also have responsibility for organizing and directing the ways in which the student works with others in school who are directly concerned with the teaching of history.

In this chapter we set out to provide practical examples of the ways in which mentors can direct, lead and coordinate the learning of history students. These examples follow a discussion of the aims, purposes and principles of mentoring, as we do not wish to fall into the trap identified by US researchers in their work on mentoring in the USA. In discussing the training offered to mentors for one programme of teacher education they say that it

> promotes a view of mentoring as a technical activity that can be controlled by applying specific strategies and techniques . . . the programme pays so little attention to mentors' own ideas about teaching and learning to teach. The training runs the risk of de-skilling mentor teachers by substituting neutral procedures for collective practical intelligence in the solution of practical problems.
> (Feiman-Nemser *et al.* 1993:152)

We have no wish to ignore the 'wisdom of practice'; quite the contrary. As we observed in Chapter 1, our argument is founded on a respect for the professional skills and knowledge of practitioners.

Aims and purposes of mentoring in history

The need for mentors in ITE has been argued from several different perspectives (McIntyre and Hagger 1993). The most persuasive argument is that traditional forms of history teacher education made relatively little use of the considerable expertise of school teachers and that the professional development of new teachers requires that beginning teachers gain access to that expertise. That expertise is seen as a distinctive form of professional knowledge and can only be provided by teachers working in their own classrooms and their own schools. The principal purpose, then, of mentoring is to find ways of ensuring that students do get access to and learn from history teachers' professional knowledge. If this is to be accomplished it demands a lot of mentors, much more than the traditional subject supervisor role. There the task was 'supervision in school, where teachers are supervising trainees in the application of training acquired elsewhere' (Maynard and Furlong 1993:71). Arranging timetables, 'lending their classes', offering practical suggestions about the best textbook on nineteenth-century Britain and about how to intoduce the feudal system, and mopping up disasters were probably the main parts of the role. This is valuable in providing a site for practising teaching, but does not fully exploit all that can be learned from the school context, and especially from the expertise of history teachers.

Much has already been written indicating the varying ways in which the role of mentor might be conceptualized generically (see, for example, Maynard and Furlong 1993; Tomlinson 1995; Brooks and Sikes 1997). Put straightforwardly, the key aspect of the mentor's role is to enable student teachers *to learn* from *teachers' expertise* as practising teachers, in *the context of school*. This key aspect indicates the principles that should underlie mentoring practices, in history as in any other subject.

Principles

The first principle is that mentoring is concerned with *student teacher learning*. Students are not in school just to practise, or to pick up suggestions, although they will be doing both, but to gradually learn about teaching and to learn to be a teacher. We have already indicated, in Chapter 2, something of what we know about the complex processes of learning to teach and here we highlight two dimensions of that learning that can inform mentors' practice. The first is that students tend initially to be concerned with themselves, and with teaching. It is only as they develop competence and confidence in their own teaching skills that they can really begin to attend to pupils' learning. The second dimension concerns their preoccupation with 'passing'; with satisfying those making assessments of them. Until they are confident that they are sufficiently competent to achieve this they are much less likely to take risks and to develop their own individual ways of being effective teachers. These two dimensions, the move from teaching history to learning, and from basic competence to autonomous development, will underlie much of what we say about ways of working with history students.

The second principle is that while they are learners, *student teachers are also adults*, and that teaching pupils history and teaching adults to teach history are not the same thing. There are, of course, similarities. The fact that both school pupils and student teachers are learners means they share certain things: they need support in their learning; they need to be challenged; they need to feel valued; and they need to know that there are high expectations of them and that they can meet those. They have individual needs and diverse skills and different things are of interest to them. Their learning is not linear, and both bring their own ideas and existing knowledge to new learning. There are important differences too. Student teachers come to teacher education with a whole range of expertise and with very well developed ideas about history, themselves as learners, about what they are here to learn, about teaching and schooling. They will be serious about what they are now embarking on and few will have made the decision lightly. Whoever they are, whatever their background, it is likely that there is a lot at stake for them in their professional education. Many will have long histories of success at school and university, and perhaps in other careers. They may find it especially hard to come to terms with the fact that they find learning to teach history extraordinarily difficult. They may also, especially if they have problems, be very well aware of their 'rights' – an increasingly common although still rare phenomenon. Most will learn well and they will learn extraordinarily quickly, although some will encounter difficulties, which may well be rooted in the preconceptions they have brought to the course. Finally, an essential difference is *what* it is these people are learning: history student teachers are engaged primarily in learning to teach history and although this will inevitably mean that they continue to learn history itself this is not the principal focus of what they are now doing. It is, however, the principal concern of history teachers working with school pupils.

The third principle is that mentors need to already have or develop particular sorts of *knowledge, skills,* and *attitudes* (Booth 1993; Kerry and Shelton-Mayes 1995; Tomlinson 1995). The most important knowledge is that which the teacher already has: of his or her own school and classes, of the history curriculum and of ways of teaching history. Mentors do not need to develop whole new bodies of knowledge about, for example, recent theories of history teaching or recent research about children's learning in history. It is, in our view, someone else's job to offer that sort of knowledge to the student (Furlong 1995). This is precisely the job that can be most effectively and efficiently provided by higher education tutors. The skills needed by mentors – listening, questioning, diagnosing strengths and weaknesses, challenging, managing time, liaising with colleagues – may look similar to those routinely practised by history teachers but they are different in this context, especially in working with an individual rather than a whole class and, unlike the knowledge base of mentoring, require development. It may be that the attitudes that are required are the most demanding of mentors: a sustained enthusiasm for teaching; a commitment to learning and to professional development; and an openness to diverse ideas about what makes an effective history teacher and history lesson.

The final principle concerns the *selection of mentors* (Berrill 1992; Shaw 1992). We recognize that there will be many history teachers who possess all the appropriate attitudes and knowledge, and perhaps the skills too, but none the less simply do not want to be mentors; their priorities lie elsewhere. There will be others who might aspire to be mentors but who have so much to learn or develop that it is doubtful if it is appropriate for them to become one. And there will be those who are known to be unsuitable but are none the less forced into the role. One of the implications of school-based teacher education, with a central role for mentors, is that schools should take the issue of the selection of mentors very seriously indeed. Headteachers need to retain an overview and ultimate responsibility for the selection and quality of mentors but the history departments will need to discuss who can best fulfil the requirements of the role (Evans 1994). Given their other responsibilities this may not be the head of department.

Table 3.1 Mentoring strategies and the dimensions of learning to teach

From teaching to learning	*From basic competence to autonomous development*

(i) An emphasis on teaching skills
   ● Example 1: Collaborative teaching
   ● Example 2: Focused observation of the mentor teaching
(ii) An emphasis on pupils' learning
   ● Example 3: Focused observation of learners
   ● Example 4: Support teaching
	(i) An emphasis on basic competence
	   ● Example 5: Structured observation of the mentor teaching
	(ii) An emphasis on autonomous development
	   ● Example 6: Critically discussing students' ideas
	   ● Example 7: Making the implicit explicit: observation and discussion of the mentor's teaching

Procedures: mentoring strategies

In our earlier discussion of student teachers' learning we indicated that there are a wide range of ways of learning to teach and about teaching. What follows is an indication of the sorts of learning opportunities that mentors can provide. Probably the most powerful opportunity for learning is the student teacher's own teaching, with discussion of that experience. As that is so central to their experience and thus to the mentor's role, we do not discuss it here; Chapter 4 is devoted to observation and discussion.

The order in which we present these other strategies relates to the dimensions of learning to teach we indicated earlier: of the move from teaching to learning, and from basic competence to autonomous development. Thus the emphasis is always on what can be learned, by the student teacher, from the strategy.

The examples, described in some detail below, are set out in Table 3.1.

From teaching to learning: (i) An emphasis on teaching skills

Example 1: Collaborative teaching

A mentor, Karen, and student, Halima, together plan the first of three lessons for Year 9 on nineteenth-century British imperialism. Before their planning meeting, Karen said that this lesson should concentrate on helping the pupils to understand what the word empire means and some of the motives for imperialism; i.e. economic, political and cultural. She indicated that subsequent lessons would look at the implications of these motives and the range of views of imperialism. Karen also provided some resources: two maps of the British Empire (one, for 1914, from an atlas, the other an illustrated 1886 version) and a selection of pictorial sources, which each suggest different motives for imperial expansion. It is early days in Halima's practice and she is keen to develop her questioning skills. They therefore create a plan that will enable the student to do this, while enabling the pupils to develop their understanding of imperialism. The outline plan that emerges from their discussion is as follows.

Mentor	Settle the class and call the register. Without an introduction, distribute to the pupils a range of objects that represent the legacy of empire, e.g. bag of sugar, a cotton T-shirt, a picture of black soldiers in the Second World War, a video of the *Jewel in the Crown*, a menu card from a Bengali restaurant, a photograph of Sydney opera house and so on. Ask the pupils: (i) what have you got; (ii) what do they all have in common? Establish that they are all evidence of the legacy of empire.
Together	Distribute maps.
Mentor	Instruct the pupils to look at these, plus the objects, to see what they can tell them about the British Empire.
Student	Lead the question and answer session following this to establish: (i) size and extent of empire; (ii) the names of particular countries; (iii) the importance of trade; (iv) political power and control.
Together	Distribute source sheets.
Mentor	Explain that having established some basic features of empire, the class will now look at why an empire was built up. The task is to examine each source, and from each identify at least one motive for empire.
Student	Lead the question and answer session to establish the following motives: (i) religious; (ii) exploration; (iii) economic; (iv) political power; (v) paternalism. While doing this, mentor will summarize these points on the board.

Mentor   Set written task: to write a paragraph saying what
the empire was and why it was built up.

Commentary The overall direction of the lesson is provided by the
mentor. Karen chooses its goal, selects appropriate resources, begins
the lesson and retains responsibility for its direction. Both at the
planning and enactment stages Halima's role is, appropriately, re-
stricted. Halima therefore has the chance to focus on the aspect of
her teaching in need of development: questioning skills, used when
the pupils have already completed a task so that there is solid and
reasonably predictable foundation for their responses. In planning
with an experienced teacher, she has the opportunity first to be
absolutely clear about the purpose of her questions and what she
wants them to achieve. She also has the chance to rehearse them
and for the mentor to suggest pupils' likely responses. Thus when
Halima suggests that she start the first set of questions with 'what
have you discovered?' Karen indicates how this might provoke
nothing or something completely unexpected about the drawing of
maps in 1886, and that a more useful approach might be focused
questions, which are more likely to lead to the answers she wants.
For example, Karen suggests that a useful question might be 'What
information do the maps provide about the size of the empire?'
Halima can try out the phrasing of specific questions involving difficult vocabulary like 'trade' or 'economic'. Karen can help her to see
that pupils may need help with these words and that alternatives
like 'buying and selling' and 'making money' may be useful.

The mentor can help the student to consider the picture sources
through the eyes of the pupils. She is able to point out that pupils
might focus on certain features of the pictures, and how Halima
might avoid becoming side-tracked by these if they are not relevant.
Equally, Karen can provide Halima with advice on prompting the
pupils to see aspects of the pictures that are important for the task.
In the lesson itself Halima has not had to worry about basic classroom management at the start of the lesson, nor the giving of
instructions for pupil tasks. Distribution of resources has been shared.
Having had the opportunity to plan the questioning very carefully,
there is every chance that it will go well and the student will gain
a sense of achievement from it. Discussion after the lesson might
focus on what it was in both the planning process and the execu-
tion of the questioning that enabled the lesson to go well, with the
intention that the student will increasingly be able to achieve these
things by planning independently, in less protected classroom contexts and in relation to more ambitious forms of questioning.

Example 2: Focused observation

The student, Mark, is to observe a lesson taught by his mentor, Katie, to a Year 10 GCSE group, following a modern world history course. The lesson is to be on the terms of the Treaty of Versailles and the reactions of Germany and the Big Three to the terms. The previous lesson concentrated on what countries might want from the settlement. Katie has planned to show a video on the treaty for the first part of the lesson, to follow this with structured note-taking on the terms and then to ask pupils to work in pairs on likely reactions to the terms of the treaty. Mark is interested in learning about two aspects of teaching: (i) the routines and rules operating more or less explicitly in the classroom; and (ii) how the teacher manages changes of activity. Before the lesson, Katie explains to Mark what she intends to do, and indicates where she thinks the main transitions in the lesson will be: starting the video; moving from that into a question and answer session accompanied by note-taking; and moving from that into paired work. She also indicates that she has particular rules about movement in the classroom, the answering of questions and how pair work is organized. Together they decide that Mark will watch for these rules to see how they work out in practice, but also to see if he can spot others that Katie hasn't mentioned. He will also watch Katie especially carefully as she comes to the end of one activity and begins the next and note what she does and says to bring about these changes.

As the pupils enter the room, Mark takes a seat slightly to the side, about half way up the classroom so that he can see both what the teacher and the pupils are doing. During the lesson he takes notes in two columns, one headed 'rules and routines' and the other 'changes of activity', although he often finds that what he writes covers both columns. He notes that when the teacher announces the video she just looks at two pupils who then pull down the blinds and that she tells the back row that they may sit on their desks. As the video comes to an end, she speaks over the end of the film telling the pupils to put the blinds up, and the rest to return to their seats and get out their notebooks. In the question and answer session that follows she only takes responses from those with their hands up and ignores anyone who calls out. He notices that as individuals finish their notes they are directed to look at relevant pages in the textbook. When she introduces the pair work she begins by summing up what has been discovered about the terms of the treaty and then gives a very clear allocation of time to the pairs; they have five minutes to work out the reactions to the terms. He notices that when they have done this she asks specific questions of pairs she identifies by name to find out what they think about the reactions. When the bell goes nobody moves until she tells them to.

Commentary If they have a chance to discuss this lesson and observation afterwards the mentor will be able to explain that the pupils who pulled down the blinds always do that: they know it is their job and she doesn't have to actually ask. That was established several weeks earlier. Similarly, she has explained to pupils that no one moves around the classroom without her permission; nor do they call out when she is asking questions. Although she does not explicitly reiterate the rule, she acts on it constantly. It also emerges that Katie has established rules about the use of their notebooks; they know to put a title and the date without being told. She also makes clear that she has established these rules – she may be able to describe how – they have not just happened.

A key point about changing activities is the teacher's prepared-ness for them. On two occasions she overlapped one activity with another so that she did not lose the class's attention, and when she wanted a distinct break she provided a time-filler for those already finished and then a clear summary of the previous activity before moving on to the next. They may also have discussed how import-ant rules and routines are to changes of activity. Such changes are accomplished much more efficiently if clear routines are established with classes. Even if the lesson could not be followed by discussion, the student will at least have learnt, by virtue of having a focus for observation, that there *are* rules and routines operating, and what some of these are. Mark will also have learnt that changes of activity do not just 'happen': they need to be directed and that there are several ways of doing this. For his next observation he could con-struct a checklist of possible rules to see, with another teacher, if these same rules operate and how they are enforced, and could add to his list of ways of bringing about changes of activity. Alternatively, he could begin to think about the rules and routines he will want to establish when he is responsible for the class, how he will establish them and why. If he is due to plan a lesson it might be that he will pay special attention to how he manages transitions in the lesson.

From teaching to learning: (ii) An emphasis on pupils' learning

Example 3: Focused observation of learners

Although Alan, the student, has been taking sole responsibility for teaching classes, he is increasingly aware that he is pitching his lessons too much towards what he feels is the middle of the ability range and that there are individuals who seem to be achieving very little. His mentor, David, agrees to teach the Year 8 class so that Alan can observe specific individuals. They agree on who these should be: Danny, who is a source of low-level disruption; Razia, for whom English is her second language; and Jeanette, who is a quiet pupil whose written work is difficult to read and understand. They agree that Alan will not intervene in the pupils' work, but will simply observe as carefully as he can throughout the lesson. He therefore sits near the front of the room where he can see them all clearly. They also agree that Alan should plan the lesson and that David will follow this as closely as he can so that the issues about which Alan is concerned are likely to emerge. The lesson is the last of a series on the English Reformation and is intended to help pupils develop an overview of the religious upheavals, and especially the shift away from Catholicism, to Protestantism, back to Catholicism and back again to Protestantism within the period 1547–62. The lesson starts with a brief recapitulation by David of religious changes in the reigns of Henry VIII, Edward VI, Mary and Elizabeth I. The teacher constructs a simple time line on the board showing reigns, dates and the words 'Catholic' or 'Protestant'. The lesson then moves on to examine the way in which these changes can be traced in the parish records of an individual church. The class look together at extracts from copies of the records for 1547, 1548 and 1549, establishing what church plate has been bought and sold and what other changes have been made. These changes are linked to the move towards Protestantism. The pupils are then told to look at the records for 1554–7 on their own and to write down at least three changes that were made to the church, together with the dates on which they were made. Once they have done this these are linked to the shift to Catholicism through teacher-led question and answer. Then the class as a whole looked at the entry for 1559 and how those changes marked a shift back. The lesson concludes with the pupils putting captions to three pictures showing the interior of the church in 1548, 1555 and 1562.

Commentary Through watching Danny, Razia and Jenny, Alan begins to notice things that he hasn't seen before. Danny actually starts the lesson looking quite interested and shouts a few answers in the initial question and answer session, but gets them all wrong: this part of the lesson is heavily dependent on memory and Danny's isn't good. Having now become bored with what is going on, Danny looks for other sources of amusement. If there was a way that the teacher could keep Danny on track for longer, there might be less trouble. Similarly he notices that when the pupils are working on their own on the church records, Danny does the first one as instructed but then seems somewhat defeated by the idea of three more. Danny's ability to concentrate emerges as a possible issue. Danny is doing more than Alan had thought, and there are some specific learning needs that he may be able to address. He is conscious though that with a topic that presents such conceptual difficulties it will be very hard to keep Danny engaged. Alan notices that although Razia volunteers nothing in the class question and answer session she is always paying attention, has an interested look on her face and certainly looks neither puzzled nor bored. It is evident that she is confused when using the textbook containing the sources and spends a lot of time whispering to her neighbour and looking at her book before she writes anything down. From watching her he considers the possibility that she may understand much more than he had previously thought, and that the problems she has are with written English rather than with understanding the Reformation. Finally, he watches Jeanette copy the table from the board (not intended by the teacher), look somewhat bemused during the question and answer session and then copy out bits of the textbook when she should be looking for changes in the church. Alan is none the wiser about her learning needs, except that he thinks they are probably very significant and perhaps he should seek some more expert help from learning support. If Alan and David can discuss the lesson afterwards Alan can have the chance to find out David's reactions to what he thinks may be the issues with Danny and Razia, and to discuss with him possible ways of changing his lessons in the future to accommodate these sorts of needs. He can also ask about the possible specialist support that Jeanette might need.

Example 4: Support teaching

Claire, the student, is already teaching effectively but knows that the goals she sets for her lessons, in terms of pupil understanding, tend to be rather vague and that she is not entirely sure what specific demands she wants to make on pupils' *historical* thinking. Her mentor, Rachel, suggests that she come and assist in a Year 11 revision lesson by working with individual pupils in order to see more closely how they respond to the work set. Rachel's lesson is on the causes of the Second World War, a topic the pupils have studied before. Rachel intends to use the lesson both to revise content and to provide pupils with practice in using cartoons as a source. Before the lesson

Rachel puts on the board a spider diagram showing seven causes: the Treaty of Versailles; the Great Depression; Japan's foreign policy; Mussolini's foreign policy; the failure of the League of Nations; Hitler's foreign policy; and the British and French policy of appeasement. Beside these are a list of relevant dates. She has also prepared a sheet of seven cartoons, each relating to one of the causes. She wants the pupils to work on their own, matching the cartoons to the events and the dates. She will then discuss this with the class before setting pupils a written task explaining how each cartoon relates to the linked cause. She recommends particular individuals with whom Claire might work during the lesson; although they usually work hard, they do not find history easy and will welcome help. She also suggests that Claire try to spend some time with a pupil who is doing extremely well and is likely to get a grade A at GCSE. At the beginning of the lesson Claire sits with one of the pupils Rachel has suggested and ends up spending most of the lesson with her. She makes a brief visit towards the end of the lesson to see how the usually successful pupil is progressing.

Commentary   Claire had thought the task of matching the cartoons to the causes would be quite difficult but she hadn't anticipated quite how hard pupils found it. Even given the information about what the causes actually were, the pupil she worked with was struggling. She matched one quite quickly, which included a statue labelled League of Nations, with the failure of the League of Nations, but when there were no such obvious clues the pupil found it very hard to read the cartoons. By helping her, Claire was able to show her how to look at every bit of the cartoons and remind her of what certain symbols meant. She was also able to prompt her in relation to using her background knowledge to decode what the cartoonist was saying. Claire became conscious that if she wanted to teach pupils to use cartoons effectively as a historical source they would need a lot of help in learning how, as it demanded a range of different sorts of skills. She also became conscious of how much she takes it for granted that pupils know that political cartoons are an incisive comment on important events. She became aware that the struggling pupil's experience of cartoons was rather different, and part of the difficulty was that she really didn't know quite what she was looking at. When she went to look at the usually successful pupil's written work towards the end of the lesson she was struck by the contrast. Although there had been a class question and answer session in between, it was clear that this pupil had few problems in making sense of the cartoon. She had been able rapidly to identify the key elements and had made good use of her background knowledge of the events. Although there was no time to discuss her observations afterwards Claire went away recognizing how demanding certain visual sources can be and how targeting the particular skills involved might help her to plan more effective lessons in the future.

From basic competence to autonomous development: (i) An emphasis on basic competence

Example 5: Structured observation

It is very early in the student's school experience, and her mentor, Jonathan, has decided that she needs to understand more about the overall structure of lessons: how the time is divided up and how a range of different activities are put together to make varying demands on the pupils. Jonathan gives Jo, the student, an observation schedule to complete as she watches his Year 8 lesson on the Black Death. Part of this is shown below. He has already filled in the class details and goals for the lesson.

Observation schedule on lesson structure

Complete the following chart at ten-minute intervals throughout the lesson. Add into the chart main changes of activity, noting the time at which they occur. After the lesson think about: (i) how the hour was divided up; (ii) what range of things pupils did during the lesson and for how long

Class: 8C   28 pupils, middle band   lesson 3 Friday 21 Nov

Aim For pupils to consider the nature of the Black Death, contemporary explanations of it and differing views of its effects on medieval society. Also for pupils to work towards an extended piece of writing on it, using a writing frame.

Time	What the teacher is doing	What the pupils are doing
10.00		
10.10		
10.20, etc.		

Commentary   By the end of the lesson, Jo has a chart, part of which looks like this:

Time	What the teacher is doing	What the pupils are doing
10.00	Asks for quiet and takes the register. Reminds them what they have done on how hard life was in medieval England.	Sitting, some chatting. Listening.
10.05	Reading bits of textbook to class about symptoms of Black Death. Asks some questions.	Listening. Some answering questions.
10.10	Still reading bits – as above.	As above.
10.15	Draws chart on board with columns for source letter and cause of Black Death. Gives pupils sources to look at and find out what each says about the causes.	Pupils copy chart outline from the board.
10.20	Going round.	Pupils reading sources and then filling in chart.

She also has brief notes about the way the lesson was divided up with about 10 minutes of input from the teacher at the beginning, then a 15-minute reading and brief writing activity by pupils working on their own. Then there was a class question and answer session for about 5 minutes on the causes. Then the pupils worked in groups for about 20 minutes to construct arguments about the extent of the effects of the Black Death. A few groups then reported back their arguments, for about 10 minutes. In thinking about what the pupils were doing, she recognized that the pupils had had to listen, read, write and discuss, for varying lengths of time, sometimes as a whole class, sometimes as individuals and sometimes in groups.

Even without discussion of the lesson, Jo will have recognized that it does have a clear structure and that the time has been carefully divided up between a range of activities. Through these activities the pupils have had to do different things and have had little time to get bored by any one of them. She may recognize that each segment of the lesson has contributed in a distinctive way to the goals for the lesson, and that this lesson will build into the next, when the pupils will be doing extended writing on the Black Death. As she begins to plan for her own teaching, she will be more conscious of the need to make decisions about the different parts of the lesson and the ways in which she might vary the demands on the pupils, and herself, at each stage.

From basic competence to autonomous development: (ii) An emphasis on autonomous development

Example 6. Critically discussing the student teacher's ideas

Gupta, the student, is over halfway through his second school placement and has had considerable success in his teaching. He is judged by all those working with him as very competent as a beginner and he is now keen to try out a range of approaches that he has used very little as yet in his teaching. One of these is IT. The history department he is working with is not keen on the use of IT in history, and despite a whole school policy on the ways in which different departments should contribute to pupils' IT capability, have resisted its introduction into their teaching. Gupta explains to his mentor, Jan, that he'd like to discuss his ideas with her and find out her reactions to the arguments presented in a university session on why IT can be valuable in history. Jan is rather nervous about all this and conscious that it is something that she is quite scared of as a teacher and tends to avoid in part because she doesn't like the idea that the pupils will be more expert than her. However, she agrees to the discussion and spends a bit of time in advance, thinking about how it might go and the sorts of issues she might raise with Gupta. Does he think that IT can make a distinctive contribution to the development of historical understanding? If so, how? What programs does he know about? Does he think history teachers, whatever their views on IT's contribution to history, should contribute to general IT capability development? What does he think are the practical issues associated with using IT here? Does he want to actually try something out with a class? What will he do? How will it fit in with the scheme of work?

Commentary Through the discussion, and particularly through Jan's questioning, Gupta begins to clarify his own thinking. He hopes that IT can make a distinctive contribution to historical thinking and that the use of certain simulation packages make possible in the classroom something that otherwise would be a nightmare to run as a single teacher alone with a group. He also recognizes from what she says that leaping in with this sort of package here may not be such a good idea: the pupils have virtually no experience of IT in history and the technician is not familiar with the software. It may be wise to work up to this, perhaps by using a word processing package in which text can be easily changed as a way of understanding how different viewpoints can be expressed. Despite Jan's obvious personal reluctance to use this herself, she has encouraged Gupta to test out his ideas in practice and has been open and honest about the ways in which these may not be the most favourable circumstances for them. She has also offered to help him in a lesson, saying that she won't be able to do much in terms of the computers but at least she can be supportive in terms of general management and discipline. Gupta now has the chance to take his ideas forward.

Example 7: Making the implicit explicit – observation and discussion of expert teaching

Maria is doing very well but is conscious that when she has been observed several teachers have commented that sometimes her lessons lack pace. She wants to learn more about how she might improve this aspect of her teaching but knows that it is far from straightforward and has found it is all too easy to end up rushing things. She asks her mentor, Irim, how she does this, but Irim finds it hard to explain beyond saying that she just feels when it's right to push on and when to slow down. Irim agrees that Maria can observe her teaching to see if through this they can identify what it is that Irim is doing. They agree that Maria will join a sixth-form lesson that Irim is teaching, and watch the first part closely so that they can discuss that afterwards in terms of pace. This is also useful because Maria has not yet done all that much A-level teaching and is due to begin a unit with the group the following week. The lesson is the first in a series on slavery and Irim intends it to involve creating an agenda for what they will be studying in the next few lessons. She wants the initial part of the lesson to involve the pupils themselves in formulating questions about slavery that are of interest to them. To achieve this she has put together a sheet, arranged in jigsaw fashion, which has on it a whole range of snippets of information about slavery: a bit of a slave auction prospectus; statistics about slaves in various states; a map of America in 1840 showing slave states; a picture of Harriet Tubman with some autobiographical information; a Negro spiritual; and so on. She begins the lesson by giving out the sheet and explaining what it contains. She asks the pupils what questions about slavery are raised for them by the information and asks them to write each of their questions on index cards, which she distributes. She then sits back and watches. After a few minutes she suddenly calls across the room to ask one of the pupils what his first question is and what has prompted it. The pupil responds and then all continue. After another few minutes she says, 'Just a few more moments. I'm always intrigued by Harriet Tubman's life'. After another few minutes she collects the cards and asks if anyone had a question about what life was like as a slave. Many of the pupils nod. She then distributes a copy of a slave testimony and says they will have a look at that to see what life might have been like. As the pupils begin to read the source, she sorts the cards she has and begins to put headings on the board based on their questions. The lesson continues.

Commentary   As she watched, Maria had been very conscious of Irim asking the sudden question to an individual and had been concerned it would break the concentration of others. She'd also been aware of Irim giving a time limit, and already knew that was useful to keep the pace up. She noticed that many of the pupils had a question about life as a slave and that therefore they were immediately interested in the slave testimony and needed little prompting to begin looking at it. As she discussed the lesson afterwards with Maria, more emerged. She asked, specifically, about why Irim had asked the initial question and Irim's response was that she had been aware that several pupils were finding it difficult to come up with questions: they had written nothing and were looking at the sheet in a rather glazed way. She knew the pupil she asked had already written down several and that he was always quite alert and would answer her question quickly and concisely, thus providing an impetus and an example to the others. Irim also said that she had deliberately thrown in the question about Harriet Tubman so they would be looking at that when she stopped them and would have a sense that there was more they wanted to find out; she felt anticipation was an important part of pace. Maria asked how she had known that they'd had long enough on the questions. Irim replied that it was a mixture of things: to some extent because they were slowing down in what they were writing; they were obviously looking in more detail at the bits of information and she felt that the task had achieved its purpose; and finally she didn't want too many questions. Finally, Maria asked about why she had used the cards for the questions, and discovered that this was so Irim could easily sort them while the pupils were reading and the lesson wouldn't be slowed down by trying to get feedback on the board or by having to sort the types of questions as they were given. The discussion focused on specifics of the lesson, and on what Irim had done and why, rather than Maria's guesses as to her motives or her views on Irim's actions, and Maria extended her understanding of pace. She recognized that in this lesson all of the following had contributed: careful planning about exactly how to do things in a way that would save time or prevent 'spaces' in the lesson; careful monitoring and picking up on cues from the pupils; use of her knowledge of individuals who could contribute to a good pace; and knowing what the responses to the material might be and building this into her plan. Maria could now try some of these out in her own teaching, especially with those classes that she knew well.

Although we have linked these opportunities for learning with a relatively simple formulation of stages or phases in learning to teach, all can be used at any stage in the student's development if they are used in different ways and with different purposes in mind. Observation by student teachers is a good example of this. Often this is used solely at the beginning of a student's experience in school as a precursor to practise, and yet student teachers repeatedly tell us that they would welcome more of it later, too, as it is only then that they are sufficiently knowledgeable about classrooms, teaching and learning to really get the most out of watching experienced practitioners at work. Similarly, collaborative teaching can provide a protected environment later in the year for the student to try out higher risk strategies like the use of simulation or drama in the history, at a time when they are increasingly concerned with the quality of pupils' learning rather than just their own teaching skills.

Managing the student's learning

We argued earlier that the mentor's task is to enable the history student teachers *to learn*, from *teachers' expertise* as practising teachers, in *the context of school*, and we have suggested a wide range of ways in which this can be done. However, if they are to fulfil their promise as learning opportunities, rather than just being experiences for the student, they will need advance planning, organizing and monitoring and this is an important part of the mentor's role (Edwards and Collison 1996). Discussion and liaison with colleagues, before students arrive and throughout their time in school, will be important elements in creating and maintaining a programme that can result in progression in learning by the student. Increasingly the student's own teaching, with regular observation and discussion of it, will dominate that programme, but all of these approaches can contribute to their learning throughout the year.

4

OBSERVATION AND DISCUSSION

Learning through their own practice is perhaps the most powerful form of learning for all student teachers (McIntyre and Hagger 1993). Our own experience with student teachers suggests as much, as do course evaluations, research evidence about what experiences students especially value and analyses of student teachers' learning. As McIntyre and Hagger note, 'beginning teachers tend seriously to underestimate the value and importance of other kinds of learning; but they are right to view their own practice as the *sine qua non* of learning to teach'; they go on to suggest that such learning, 'is generally much more effective if it is supported by a competent, experienced practitioner' (McIntyre and Hagger 1993:90). Similarly, in their systematic evaluation of the perceived value of different activities associated with particular roles in a teacher education programme, Rothwell *et al.* found that 95 per cent of ex-students rated highly their mentor's contribution to observing their teaching and providing feedback (Rothwell *et al.* 1994). The central importance of this sort of activity is well established. It is a process designed for and carried out to contribute to student teachers' learning. Making judgements about the quality of teaching and learning, and about the outcomes of particular lessons and learning activities, may be elements in observation and discussion but they are not the central concern of the activities. In this respect at least, observation and discussion of student teachers' work in classrooms are fundamentally different from the sorts of classroom observations that lie at the heart of the Office for Standards in Education (Ofsted) inspection process or some versions of the appraisal of experienced teachers (Elliott 1989; Ofsted 1995).

The aims and purposes of observation and discussion

The primary purpose of observation and discussion is to support students' learning and in particular to *enhance their skills in the classroom*, be they generic or subject specific, to develop an *understanding* of their practice and the rationale underlying it and to learn *how to evaluate* their own teaching (McIntyre 1994; Hagger *et al.* 1995; Barton and Elliott 1996). The first concerns the student's capacity *to perform particular classroom activities more effectively*. Focuses for improvement might be generic classroom skills such as in: giving instructions; distributing resources; asking questions; using the white board; organizing pupils into groups; and concluding a lesson. They may, equally, be subject-related, concerned with skills in deploying historical language or helping learners to acquire particular historical concepts and ideas. Where students are helped to recognize what they are currently doing, and to understand the effects of those actions, and are offered further suggestions for practice it is likely that they will learn to do all these sorts of things better in the future. In this respect, observation and discussion are primarily concerned with classroom practice and with change. The second purpose of observation – to develop an *understanding* of their practice and the rationale underlying it – depends on *shared experience of what is happening in students' lessons*. It is likely that only through observation and discussion, for example, will a student see that although some pupils were able to understand the term communism from the explanation, for others further activities were necessary, or that the task set for group work about the role of war in the development of medicine was actually much better done than the student had originally thought. In discussing what they have done, students can be encouraged to think about not just how they did things but also what they did and why. In this respect, observation and discussion, in the hands of skilled and experienced teachers, can help to develop students' understanding of the learning process and the needs of pupils. Finally, skilled observation and effective discussion can help students to learn *how to evaluate* their own teaching. They can learn that the questions they are asked about how they did things, why they did them and whether or not they were worth doing, are important ones, and that seeking answers can enhance their practice and their *thinking about that practice*.

As we saw in Chapter 3 there are a range of learning opportunities that mentors can set up for students but with the exception of collaborative teaching, the combination of skilful observation and discussion is the only strategy that can contribute so much to students' learning and to all the goals that we have set for ITE. Observation and discussion also have an important diagnostic function for both mentor and student (Hagger *et al.* 1995). They play a major part in establishing what it is that needs to be learned and what the priorities for learning should be. A student, for example, may feel satisfied that pupils have been very involved in her lesson about Hitler's rise to power, that her improved management skills brought this about and that she has little more to learn about this. Her perceptions were based on the fact that the previous lessons about the collapse of the Weimar Republic were poorly managed and her own evaluations suggested that poor management contributed to work of inferior quality. Observation and discussion of the lesson may help the student to recognize that although all the pupils were very busy and did all the tasks, and that this was an important achievement in the context of recent lessons, they were not really involved in the historical ideas and that the next lesson should concentrate on ensuring that sort of involvement through more active questioning focused on the key historical ideas. Another student may be conscious that intermittent low-level disruption such as general chatter is common in his Year 10 lessons on the American West, but has no real idea why. A skilled observer may be able to help him to recognize that in one lesson at least it is pace that is the issue – slow writing on the board during a feedback session about the uses of the buffalo by native Americans, lengthy distribution of resources on Sioux belief systems, not being quite sure how to give instructions for the follow-on activity about ancestor worship – and that if he can learn how to tighten up on these things in future lessons the low level disruption may disappear.

Given its diagnostic function it follows that the nature of the observation and the nature of the discussion will vary depending on what is to be learned. Earlier in the year it is likely to focus on the students' own actions and be strongly directed by the mentor, who will use their expertise to influence the students' priorities and help them to recognize, for example, that until they give instructions clearly (and have been offered ways of doing this) there will always be confusion in the lesson. As students develop competence it is likely that they will be increasingly able to determine for themselves what they want and need to learn from this process and the pupils' learning can become a priority. Effective mentors will be aware of this transition – indeed they will have helped it come about – and will adjust observation and discussion accordingly.

Principles underpinning observation and discussion

Evidence and experience suggest that there are six main principles that should inform observation and discussion of the student's teaching if they are to be most effective in enabling them to learn.

Teaching is so complex that students simply cannot, in their learning, attend to everything at once: observation and discussion must be *focused and specific*. Focusing on specific aspects will help them to both understand what the constituent parts are and to gradually develop their skills. Although they may actually be trying, simultaneously, to ask open questions, involve the quiet girls at the side, inject enthusiasm into their voices and use non-verbal cues to quell the troublemaker, concentrating on just one or two of these in observation and discussion is much more likely to lead them to make progress in developing that skill. The demands of learning to teach and about teaching are such that it will be overwhelming unless they concentrate on just some of it at any one moment. What the nature of the focus is will probably be influenced by three sorts of considerations: the student's learning needs, as perceived by the mentor; the same needs as perceived by the student; and the official agenda of what they need to learn – the course requirements and the sort of lesson that the student is teaching. There is probably little point, for example, in choosing as a focus the ways in which the student motivates and interests the pupils if the lesson is about iron and steel and the mentor knows that no teacher has ever succeeded in motivating pupils on that topic. An implication of what we have said so far is that focus is determined in advance of observation, and the observation is guided by it. Thus the observer is not there just to 'look at everything' or 'how it goes generally' or just to pick up on whatever turns out to be memorable in the lesson. Instead the observer is there to contribute in a planned and systematic way to the student's learning. For example, in order to develop a particular student's classroom effectiveness a mentor might need to focus not on 'teacher talk' in a lesson about the Russian Revolution, but on the phrasing of questions and students' response to pupil answers. Rather than focusing on 'pupil interest' in the topic of the Romano-British villa, a mentor might need to centre observation on the questions pupils ask, the time they take to begin tasks and the quality of pupil–pupil discussion.

The ideas of focus and specificity also imply the notion of *selectivity*, not only in terms of what is to be observed but also in relation to the discussion afterwards. Even with a tight focus there is usually so much that could be said that again there is a real danger of overwhelming the student with a too extensive agenda for discussion. Deciding on priorities is a demanding task and will depend on a range of factors. For example, if a student's questioning on the Russian Revolution has provoked very little response from the pupils, and the student's responses to these few pupil answers has been negative and critical, the mentor should choose to focus on one issue; perhaps the phrasing of the questions or ways of being positive about the pupils' answers. In practice, the choices are more complex than this, and mentors will select items for feedback depending on the student's capacity for learning, the time available, and the opportunities for developing particular classroom skills. Selectivity in observation and discussion is especially important when a student's classroom skills are extremely poor.

Given the complexity of learning to teach and the force of observation and discussion as a means for learning it should be undertaken *frequently*. Obviously students need the chance to develop the sorts of relationships they want and to face the challenge of teaching without the effects of the presence of the normal class teacher. That said they should probably be observed about once a week with each of the classes for which they have assumed responsibility. This will vary depending on particular timetables, students and schools but that level of frequency is appropriate and should continue throughout the year. There is a real danger of leaving a student alone because 'there's no problem here'. However skilled a student, he or she can always learn more, and open discussion with a mentor about his or her teaching, which has as its starting point a shared experience of a lesson, will always be valuable.

Mentors are in a particularly strong position to be well informed about a student's progress and to use this as a way of directing observation and discussion; observation and discussion must be *progressive*. Frequent use of observation and discussion means that each occasion can have a link with the next, so that over time a full range of issues can be addressed. Mentors can direct a student's development over the course of a series of lessons with the same class, noting elements of progression and being alert to any new priorities. Having worked with a student to address difficulties in questioning techniques in teaching the Russian Revolution, a mentor is in a position subsequently to help the student address issues related to the pupils' understanding of the concept of 'communism'. If such progression is to be achieved it will be valuable to ensure that the end of any discussion of observed teaching includes a setting of targets and a way forward; what the student will concentrate on next and what opportunities there will be for that learning. If occasions for observation and discussion are isolated experiences and are excessively judgemental they are much more likely to have the flavour of Ofsted visits. It is one of the ways in which the mentor is so much better placed than any university or higher education tutor visiting the student. However frequent their visits they will never be able to take account of the fine detail of progress in the ways that the mentor's work with the student can.

Students are most likely to learn from discussions of observed lessons where the discussion is framed in *positive* terms which focus on what has been achieved and what needs to be achieved next. The difficulty is that it seems that *all* observers have a tendency to be critical or negative about what they have seen. Natural reactions to negative criticism include defensiveness, anger, a sense of unfairness and a desire to find reasons or excuses for the 'failure'. Most beginning teachers are trying to do their best and will have thought long and hard about their lessons. Many are lacking in confidence both in and out of the classroom, although they may be very good, as adults, at hiding this. It is only where mentors focus on the positive aspects of what has been achieved that students will feel the confidence to continue to develop. Paradoxically, it can be the case that it is precisely the mentor's desire to help a student to achieve that produces a negative discussion. Lesson observations prompt any number of, 'If only he had . . .' thoughts and the discussion can become a catalogue of negative criticism. Such discussions can destroy what little confidence a student has, and make it very hard for the student to 'hear' what is being said, however justified and reasonable it may be. This means that all debriefing discussions should concentrate on what went well before what went badly, on strengths before weaknesses and on achievements before areas for development, and should ensure agreement on clear realistic targets and ways of achieving them. In saying that the experience should be positive we are not suggesting a lack of honesty about what the student did or did not achieve. However, if the student is to accept legitimate criticism and act on suggestions, these need to be understood. Such understanding is much more likely to be achieved in a context in which students' efforts are valued, where they believe they can make progress and where they can see a way forward.

Observation and discussion must be *two-way*. We have deliberately tried to avoid using the word 'feedback' in writing about discussion of students' teaching. This is because it seems to imply that after the lesson the purpose of the conversation is simply for the mentor to tell the student what he or she thought about the lesson, and the chosen focus. While we think it very important that the mentor does give an opinion and offer suggestions for ways of improving practice, these should emerge as part of a conversation about the lesson in which the student's views of it need to be the starting point. If the student's views do not emerge early on it will be very hard for the mentor to gauge what to say or to know how to be selective. It is clearly preferable where a mentor's commentary emerges through skilful questioning or the discussion of non-judgemental information about what actually happened. In these circumstances, when a student has not simply been told the mentor's view, he or she is far more likely to be able to understand and accept it.

The principles we have outlined may sound unrealistic for mentors. Practical experience suggests that they are not. Effective mentors are also skilful at knowing what is realistic and feasible in their particular circumstances. They know that any lessons they observe on a Tuesday, for example, will only ever be followed by a brief discussion because they have full teaching loads that day. Hence the focus chosen for those lessons is always highly specific and very limited so that it can be discussed in just a few minutes. They know that one of their colleagues is often tempted to just leave the student on their own. Thus they ensure that on a regular basis they specifically ask that colleague to observe particular parts of a lesson and they give them the focus for the observation. They know that one of their colleagues finds it very hard not to come across as overly critical, so they ask that colleague to work on developing one of the student's strengths. They know that they themselves have a tendency to leap in and start talking too much, and hence force themselves to wait for the student to talk about the achievements of the lesson.

Procedures: from principles to practice

How might these principles translate into practice? In what follows, we discuss two examples of students' history lessons and what might be involved in the observation and discussion of these. We know that in many ways these examples will appear artificial: readers do not know the students, their recent experiences and backgrounds and the contexts of the school. Important concerns, such as classroom layout and resource availability, cannot be addressed, and the plans for the lessons are presented as the unproblematic outcomes of decision-making processes. None the less we suggest that these lessons, carefully dissected, can illuminate the process of observation and discussion in the development of history teachers.

The two lessons here are presented first through their plans. This is a useful and important reminder that the plan is an essential piece of evidence in the observation. Even if, for whatever reason, elements of the plan are not subsequently implemented, the plan indicates how the student *wanted* the lesson to go. The plan indicates the decisions about teaching that have already been made. If the plan is an important aid to effective observation and discussion there are two other technical aids that should not be overlooked. Cassette recorders are excellent for exploring some elements of classroom interaction, especially teacher talk. They are less effective for hearing pupils talk, except in small groups. None the less, they are generally unobtrusive. Video cameras provide infinitely richer data, but are, of course, more obtrusive. There is a strong case for *insisting* that all student teachers are videoed teaching on several occasions. The lesson can be re-run in discussion sessions to focus on key ideas and key points. Use of freeze-framing can open up discussion about other possible ways of developing any given idea or classroom situation. Finally, and importantly, for the student videotapes can provide tangible evidence of progression in competence and attainment as a teacher, even if many students will shudder when asked to watch tapes of their early teaching efforts!

Before introducing the two lessons, it might be useful to identify the issues that need to be confronted and resolved by mentors as points of procedure in translating the principles underpinning observation and discussion into practice. In particular, it is useful to highlight the issues that need to be confronted and resolved by mentors and students at three stages of the process of observation and discussion: before the lesson; during it; and in the discussion afterwards. These are covered in the following list of questions for mentors.

Issues for mentors in observation and discussion

Before the lesson

1 What is the focus to be and how will this be decided?
   - How will you take account of what you know about the student's progress and what he or she thinks about it?
   - How relevant will the course goals be in selecting the focus?
   - What effect does the nature of the lesson planned have on the choice of focus?
   - What effect does the nature of the teaching group have on the choice of focus?
   - How will the time for the discussion affect the choice of focus?

2 What are the ground rules for observation in this particular lesson?
   - Is there to be a discussion about the lesson plan? Will you suggest changes?
   - What do you need to know about the student's intentions if you are to observe what's been agreed?
   - What form will your observation take?
   - Will you write anything down?

During the lesson

1 Practical issues
   - Where will you sit? Will you remain in the same place throughout, and will your choice of position allow you to address the focus of the observation?
   - Will you be working with individual pupils or with a group or remain a relatively 'detached' observer?
   - Will you be watching the student or the pupils, and how will you decide which at each stage of the lesson?
   - What sorts of things will you be noting (in your head, on paper)?

2 Intervention
   - Will you intervene, and if so under what circumstances?
   - Will you wait for the student to ask?
   - Will you have conversations with the student during the lesson?
   - What will you do if things get out of hand?
   - Are you specifically observing for part of the lesson and helping individuals for the rest?

After the lesson

1 The process of discussion
   - When and where will the discussion take place, and for how long?
   - What practical constraints (e.g. other lessons, departmental and school meetings) are there?
   - Who will start the talking?
   - What should be the balance of you and the student speaking or listening?
   - What should you concentrate on in your suggestions?
   - What if the lesson went seriously wrong?
   - What if you can't think of any ways that the student could have done better?
   - What will be the conclusion of the discussion?
   - What do you want the student to take away from it?

2 Outcomes
  • What will happen next?
  • What, if any, written outcome will there be?
  • Are there issues to do with confidentiality about the recording and reporting of the outcomes? Can they be resolved? What if there is substantial disagreement?

Lesson 1: Witchcraft lesson for Year 8, early in the student's year

Lesson plan

Class 8K   13 February 1997   lesson 4 11.45–12.35

Aim To gain an understanding of the belief in witchcraft in Tudor and Stuart times, in particular the types of people that were accused of being witches, using a variety of primary and secondary sources.
Key elements   2a (beliefs and attitudes of people); 4a (using a range of sources of information); and 5c (communicate knowledge and understanding using a range of techniques).
Resources   Overhead Projector (OHP) – OHT on witches. Information sheet. Source sheet. Dialogue.

Beginning of the lesson (5 mins)   Hand back students' books and work sheets. Show OHT of a witch. Ask students to guess what the lesson is about. Hold a lighter to a students' hand asking if it is hot. Explain that in the seventeenth century you would be burned alive if you were found guilty of being a witch.

Main activities
  • (5 mins) Ask some students to read aloud the information sheet. Stop to draw out important points and make links with their previous study.
  • (10 mins) Ask students to look at sources sheet. Working in pairs they should examine the sources and draw up a list of characteristics of the types of people most often accused of being witches.
  • (10 mins) Ask two students to read through a dialogue between two women in the seventeenth century about someone they suspect is a witch. Ask students to tell me about the characteristics of a witch. Write these on the board.
  • (15 mins) Explain task. Arrange this information into diagrammatic form, with the title, 'How to spot a witch'. Suggest ways

of doing this; e.g. picture clues of a hat, a familiar, flow chart, spider diagram.

End of lesson (5 mins)   Ask students why people aren't accused of being witches today. Pack away. Hand in sheets.

Extension work   Which sources are primary? Which sources are secondary?
Board work   Date and title; 'How to spot a witch'. Instructions for diagram.

Without knowing anything of the context, the plan itself does suggest that the student has already learned a considerable range of issues to do with planning, teaching and classroom management and also suggests a range of areas for subsequent development:

- Although the goal or aim for the lesson is expressed in terms of the pupils, it is somewhat vague. There is no indication of what 'understanding belief' might mean. There are also questions about the relationship between the goal and the planned activities in the lesson. All of this suggests a student at a relatively early stage of development.
- The student has clearly learnt about the importance of structuring a lesson, with a planned beginning and end, and with a series of defined activities or tasks. The mentor might want to ask about the links between the activities, the relationship of one task to another and the relationship between all of these and the aim for the lesson.
- The lesson is relatively unproblematic in terms of classroom management. Teacher activity mainly consists of giving instructions. In so far as there is interaction between the teacher and the pupils it is mostly limited to a question and answer session on a task already completed by the pupils. Greater interaction between teacher and taught could be a focus for the future once confidence has been gained.
- There is a variety of pupil tasks: the student recognizes the need to make a range of demands on them and involve them in doing different sorts of things during the lesson: listening; reading; analysing; and discussing.

All of these features suggest a student who is learning well but is still concentrating most on his or her own needs as a teacher rather than on the pupils as learners: goals are related to the subject, and the lesson is conceived in managerial terms. In the light of that, the following might be appropriate in the observation and discussion.

Before the lesson

Deciding the focus for observation and discussion   Although it might seem that the issues of the overall coherence of the lesson and the relationship between this and the lesson's goals are the most pressing issues to consider here, if this student is at a relatively early stage in his or her development it is probably more important to focus on what he or she will be doing in the lesson, and choose as a focus some aspect of his or her actions. As the lesson involves several sets of giving instructions, it could be that this would be the most appropriate focus. Thus it is the student's stage of development and the nature of the lesson plan that have determined the choice of focus.

Decisions about the form of the observation   If the giving of instructions provides the main focus for observation, there are probably two main ways in which these could be observed. The mentor could try to note down instructions given by the student and the pupils' response to these. Alternatively, once an activity has started the mentor might work with pairs of students to see if they understand what they have to do and how to do it. The first of these will almost certainly need some written record (although a cassette recorder or video camera would make it possible to focus on pupil reactions), whereas it will not be easy to keep a record of the second while it is actually happening. The mentor might, though, jot down any questions that pupils ask about what they are supposed to be doing once they have started.

Discussion of the plan itself   Although the lesson's coherence could be discussed this seems inappropriate shortly before it is to be taught. It would probably require some major reorganization to be made more coherent. But it might be appropriate to air reservations about one activity, perhaps the first 'starter' activity which is a 'hook' for the lesson, and to suggest an alternative that might engage pupil interest.

During the lesson

Provided there has been a reasonably full discussion beforehand then observation during the lesson should, in principle, be straightforward. However, if pupils are unclear about what they should be doing with their diagrams, should the mentor intervene to explain or, perhaps, go to tell the student that many pupils seem unclear but make no specific suggestion about what to do? If the pupils' lack of comprehension is accompanied by references to the student – 'We never understand when —— explains things. She doesn't make it clear' – then difficulties might arise. Given the early stage of the year, an important issue is not to undermine the student in any way and certainly not to collude with the pupils, even if they are right. It may be worth while to help some individuals, using a phrase such as, '—— asked you to . . .'; rephrasing the instruction so that it will be clear. Perhaps equally problematic are the observer's reactions to pupil misbehaviour. There are few general principles, except that pupils' safety is paramount, but it is useful to have clarified before the lesson the circumstances under which intervention might occur. If student and mentor have worked closely together then it is unlikely that the relationship will be disrupted by unforeseen circumstances suddenly being a problem, but it will always need to have been sorted out at some stage.

After the lesson

Hagger *et al.* (1995:61) outline guidance on the structure that conversations following lesson observations might follow. Table 4.1 adapts their model to this particular lesson.

Although in the example in Table 4.1 the student is extremely responsive, less responsive students can be helped to consider the lesson when presented by the observer with examples of how they phrased instructions or specific questions asked by pupils. Good practice in these discussions is characterized by dialogue rather than by mentors 'telling' students what was effective or less successful.

This observation and discussion will need a written outcome. In this case, two sorts of record would probably be appropriate: one created by the student and another by the mentor. The student's might include a note of specific suggestions made and perhaps what to avoid in the future, whereas the teacher's might include any notes taken in the lesson itself plus a very brief summary, created during the discussion, of strengths, areas for development and future targets. The mentor's record should be kept both by the mentor and the student. Such records will develop into a portfolio that can be used to review progress and subsequently make summative judgements of competence.

Table 4.1   Structure for conversation following lesson observation.

Participant	Conversation	Aim
Mentor	Makes positive comment about the lesson. General: 'I did enjoy that', 'All the preparation paid off then'. Specific: 'It was good to see you got Jamie reading at the beginning, he hasn't done that before', 'those sources you chose were really interesting – where did you find them?'	Help the student to feel that there is something to be valued in what they have done.
Mentor	Asks general open question: 'How did you feel it went?'; 'What were you pleased with?'	Start by finding out how the student feels about the lesson.
Student	Talks about strengths of the teaching in terms of the focus chosen: 'I was pleased by the fact that I got several volunteers to read the sheet at the beginning and I don't think they felt too interrupted by me. I think I made it clear that I'd want to stop them at times. But I wasn't too sure that they got what I wanted about characteristics of the witch from the sources – did they ask you many questions about that?'	Try to get the student to discuss strengths as fully as possible and what contributed: 'Maybe you got volunteers because you asked in a really nice way – you said, "Who's going to help me? Who would like to read this bit for us?" And maybe they didn't mind being interrupted because you told them first that you would so they weren't surprised.' Try to avoid letting the student get on to 'weaknesses' until the strengths have been fully explored: 'Yes, I think you're right there, but let's think about the diagram – they all got on with that quickly which is a good indicator that they knew what to do. What do you think helped there?'

Table 4.1   *(cont'd)*

Participant	Conversation	Aim
Mentor	Asks a specific question about an aspect that needed development: 'What about the instructions for using the sources – what made you think that they weren't so good?'	Encourage the student to identify the cues pupils may have given – to analyse what was happening.
Student	Begins to unpick these and suggests how they may have contributed: 'I heard them ask you questions, and I saw some puzzled looks on faces. Was what I said too vague? Did they understand "characteristics"?'	Student begins to identify for themselves what might not have been appropriate: the need for specificity; the need for appropriate vocabulary; perhaps the need to have rehearsed the instructions.
Mentor	Confirms (or not) the student's suggestions and offers more alternatives: 'Make sure they all look at you before you start with the instructions'; 'Make sure they all know which sheet you are talking about'; 'Maybe do an example with them'; 'Ask a pupil to say back to you what they are going to do.'	Give the students suggestions for practice that they can use on another occasion, and ensure the student notes these down.
Mentor and student	Decide where to go next: more concentration on instructions? Or moving on to, say, the issue of the links between activities in the lesson.	Make plans for the future and set targets.

Lesson 2: Introduction to medieval realms for Year 7

Lesson plan

Class: 7J   6 February 1997   lesson 2 9.45–10.35

Topic   Introduction to medieval realms.

Aims   To provide pupils with an overview of the main features and developments of the Middle Ages (2c: overviews of a period) and to motivate them about a new study unit.

Pre-lesson and resources   Board work: title and pictures, page numbers from books. Books: *Past into Present, History Scene*. Handouts: title-page designs. Audio tapes (two), video cued up, adaptor plug, crayons, rulers.

Beginning of lesson (5 mins)
1 Pupils enter to medieval music.
2 Teacher explanation: new unit, medieval realms (Middle Ages).

Tasks and activities
1 Question and answer session (5 mins). Using pictures on the board, elicit from pupils what aspects of medieval Britain they will study.
2 Sound effects (5 minutes). Teacher plays, pupils guess (a) what the sounds are (b) where they would have heard them.
   (i) Sound 1: plainchant
   (ii) Sound 2: boiling oil from castle
   (iii) Sound 3: torture.
3 Visual stimuli.
   (i) Castles (5 mins). Using books, pupils look at pictures. Ask, 'What are some of the different styles of castle that were built? Have you visited a castle? What interested you?'
   (ii) Knights (5 mins). Watch video clip. Ask, 'Tell me three different games that knights are playing at the tournament.'
   (iii) Churches (5 mins). Using books. Ask, 'What differences are there between the churches?' (play plainchant during this).
4 Set task. Design title-page for medieval realms unit. To be completed for homework.

End of lesson   Collect in books – pass to end of rows. Sum up lesson.

This is clearly an ambitious lesson and the student has obviously spent considerable time planning it. It suggests that in many ways he or she is skilled in the classroom, and will be able to orchestrate the wide range of resources which he or she is planning to deploy. In contrast with the previous lesson, it is demanding of the student and requires considerable confidence on his or her part. Given all that, it suggests that this student may be ready to think hard about pupils' learning and the outcomes of what he or she does in those terms.

Before the lesson

Deciding the focus for observation and discussion   One of the aims of the lesson is affective – to motivate the pupils – and it seems highly likely from the plan that if the student can accomplish what he or she intends then this will be achieved. The other aim is more problematic since it is difficult to establish what is meant by pupil understanding of overviews (Riley 1997). Given the conceptual challenge of the lesson and the student's apparent strength, observation could focus on the extent to which the lesson achieves both its affective and cognitive goals.

Decisions about the form of the observation   Part of the purpose of the observation may simply be to explore the lesson in subsequent discussion with the student so that its outcomes can be assessed together. The observer could also collect information that will relate to the pupils' motivation: how quickly they settled to the tasks; their willingness to ask unprompted questions; their sustained concentration. The use of a video camera might capture less tangible evidence: the looks on their faces; the behaviour and reactions of particular pupils. The observer could also collect information about what the pupils seem to be making of the material: what comments do they make about what happens? An important piece of evidence will be the products of pupil work, for example, what they include on the title-pages they construct at the end of the lesson.

Discussion of the plan itself   It may well be that there is little to be discussed at this stage, since this is a confidently constructed plan, other than checking that the student has actually amassed the various resources and asking if he or she needs any help with them during the lesson. It might be appropriate to ask about contingency plans if the pupils become overexcited.

During the lesson

The only difficulty may be that a lesson as potentially interesting as this one involves the observer so much in it that he or she loses the slight distance needed if pupils are to be carefully observed, especially when the intention is to look at their response in terms of the somewhat sophisticated history in the lesson.

After the lesson

The format suggested by Hagger *et al.* (1995) (Table 4.1) is again useful. The discussion might start with the student identifying the strengths of the lesson and the mentor adding any other apparent successes, before the mentor starts to unpack possible areas for development, make suggestions, and end with targets for the future. Here, discussion might focus on how well the lesson motivated pupils. Indicators of motivation will need to be identified, and consideration given to what elements of the design and implementation of the activities and tasks led to this. Discussion of the aim to 'provide pupils with an overview of the main features and development of the Middle Ages' might begin by asking the student what he or she thinks the pupils will have taken away from the lesson. The most likely response is that they will know that castles, knights, churches and torture were all characteristic of the period. It may be that the nature of architectural change in castles and churches will also have emerged and that the student will believe that pupils have therefore grasped the concept of development within the period. This could lead on to a discussion of whether or not this is what the student meant by the concept of an 'overview', the ways in which this might be similar or different to that intended in the national curriculum order (DfEE 1994) and what alternative versions there might be. Such discussion might broaden into a consideration of the ways in which teachers might assess the utility of 'overviews' as a teaching tool. A possible way of concluding this discussion might be to return to what was achieved in terms of motivation and the possibility that that might have sufficed as a goal in itself, since success in this regard would contain benefits for future lessons with the class. Future targets might relate to clarity of goals for future lessons; what the student really means by them and how each part of the lesson will relate to those goals.

In both of the lessons discussed above the assumption has been that the mentor directs the student's progress and has a major part to play in deciding on the focus, directing the discussion – albeit through questions rather than statements – making suggestions for future practice and deciding on future targets. As training proceeds, the student will have an increasing input into such discussions but none the less the mentor is, quite rightly, the one who is directing the learning. We suggest that towards the end of training this should change in emphasis as the student becomes a *competent beginner*. Once students have shown that they can achieve what is required of them as a beginner they should be encouraged to take responsibility for directing their own learning as far as possible. At this stage it should be the student who sets the focus, in terms of what he or she wants to achieve as a teacher, and the student who should be drawing the conclusions in post-lesson discussion. Students will probably still need mentors' opinions and ideas but these should be to help students develop their own perspectives.

If learning to teaching is complex so too is learning how to help someone learn to teach. We have indicated in this chapter that although effective mentoring through observation and discussion is grounded in the everyday world of the classroom and in teachers' professional skills as planners and evaluators of teaching and learning, a range of skills and practices need to be developed. Both the examples we have worked through indicate how good mentors combine their understanding of context, their expertise in teaching and their awareness of a students' development to support the emergence of secure competence.

5

ASSESSMENT

An underlying theme of our discussions of ways in which mentors can work with student teachers has been that the choice of learning opportunities and the directions they take, depend on continuous evaluation of a student's progress. Judgements need to be made about what should come next in students' experience if their development is to continue. This process of continuous evaluation is often referred to as *formative assessment,* and is a key aspect of the work of mentors. Although closely linked to the process of summative assessment, in which final judgements are made about the student's competence, there are distinctions between the two. Other writers have described these distinctions thus: 'evaluation is both ongoing and implicit in all mentoring acts. Assessment happens periodically when one pauses to take stock of the evaluative process, makes it more explicit, identifies and justifies judgements which are made and reports conclusions' (Crosson and Shiu 1995:110). Brooks and Sikes observe that,

> formative assessment is a dynamic process aimed at propelling students towards teaching competence. The evidence gained in this ongoing process contributes to the summative assessment, which is a more formal summing up of progress-to-date, which may occur at more than one point during the course and ultimately at the end of the course when pass/fail decisions have to be made.
>
> (Brooks and Sikes 1997:126)

In this chapter our concern moves from *formative assessment* as a basis for the identification of future development needs to summative assessment; making a judgement of the student's progress and achievements and summarizing these in a formal report.

Aims and purposes of summative assessment

Ultimately the purpose of summative assessment in initial teacher education is to decide who should be awarded Qualified Teacher Status (QTS). To make that judgement, students have to be assessed against criteria that, however expressed, represent what are seen to be the 'professional characteristics' and 'professional competencies' of a successful teacher (Whitty 1996:89). As we indicated in Chapter 2, there has been much debate as to what those criteria should be, how they should be expressed and what assumptions are embedded in the chosen formulation (see, for example, McCulloch and Fidler 1994; Hustler and McIntyre 1996). Increasingly over the past decade, summative assessment criteria in teacher education have been developed as statements of outcome competence, which set out to define what newly qualified teachers should know, understand and be able to do in the classroom. The current statutory requirements are set out in the *Standards for the Award of Qualified Teacher Status* (DfEE 1997a).

This concern with outcome competencies is relatively new in teacher education, although it has been common in other professions for some time (Elliott *et al.* 1986; Elliott 1995; Schostak and Phillips 1995). In education, there have been a number of competing, and shifting, attempts to define competency frameworks (DfE 1992, 1993). Some commentators have suggested that competence-based frameworks are unhelpful in teacher education. Their argument is that few teaching situations, and few teaching abilities, are easily reducible to simple competence statements, and that the use of such competence frameworks restricts rather than supports the development of professional growth, whereas differences between schools and classrooms, let alone subjects, make such frameworks self-defeating at best (Norris 1991; Stronach *et al.* 1996). Others argue that although few competence statements can capture the complexities of the classroom, some statement of outcomes is useful both for students and mentors in defining realistic goals and expectations (Whitty 1996).

The current statutory requirements are certainly daunting, with 46 separate statements of competence organized under four headings: knowledge and understanding; planning, teaching and classroom management; monitoring, assessment, recording, reporting and accountability; and other professional requirements (DfEE 1997a). The range is considerable. Some of the standards are concerned with elements of professional and subject knowledge. For example, newly qualified teachers must, 'have a secure knowledge and understanding of the concepts and skills in their specialist subject at a standard equivalent to degree level to enable them to teach it confidently and accurately through the secondary school' (A1(i)) as well as an understanding of national curriculum and examination syllabus requirements (A1(ii)), but also knowledge of the statutory framework within which education operates, such as the implications of the Race Relations Act (1976), the Children Act (1989) and the various Education Acts of the past decade (Da(ii)). Others are to do with classroom pedagogy, set out in some detail so that newly qualified teachers must have demonstrated the ability, for example, to 'ensure effective teaching of whole classes, of groups and individuals within the whole class setting, so that teaching objectives are met and best use is made of available teaching time' (Bf), and 'to use teaching methods which ensure . . . effective questioning which matches the pace and directions of the lesson and ensures that pupils take part' (Bk(vi)). Yet others make assumptions about the nature of the teaching profession, so that newly qualified teachers must 'be aware of and know how to access recent inspection and research evidence' (A(ix)).

As an attempt to list the characteristic actions of and responsibilities of the classroom teacher, the national standards are certainly compendious, and it is difficult to object to any of the *individual* standards. In this respect, moreover, they stand as a reminder of the complexity of the teachers' task, and the expectations we have that new teachers will enter the profession with skills and knowledge in their subject, in classroom pedagogy and in assessment methods and issues at a sophisticated level. However, taken as a whole the national standards present difficulties for students and mentors. There is little explicit guidance on the *links* between different elements of the standards, and little indication of the significance of classroom contexts in shaping what it is that teachers are frequently able to do. There is little explicit attention to the complexity of pupil learning, other than through the importance of students' learning about the need to provide for the individual needs of all learners, and no reference to the ways in which teaching may be only one of a number of factors influencing the extent to which pupils learn. Moreover, the sheer length of the list of standards creates difficulties on both sides. For mentors, there are issues to do with the selection of learning targets at different stages of training. For example, it may be that, for some students, issues to do with pupil assessment should simply be set aside while issues to do with questioning are addressed. For students, too, the length of the list is daunting – at least one of us has had the experience of working through the current list of national standards with head teachers who decided that they, as expert members of the profession, were incapable of meeting expectations!

Taken as a whole then, the standards may help to 'map' the nature of the teacher's task, but they are unhelpful as an assessment document. Most mentors will be working in courses where the national standards have been adapted to render them more usefully assessable and where agreement has been reached between the higher education institution and its partner schools on which standards might be addressed at each stage of the year and under what circumstances. This sort of selection is essential, but it should not entirely preclude the possibility of mentors and students together selecting items for assessment that are seen as problematic or challenging.

Interim summative assessment

Most, if not all, programmes of teacher education require summative assessments not just of the final outcomes but also at intermediate stages; at the end of each school placement, or at defined points during a placement, for example. It is relatively rare for there to be explicit clarity about quite what is expected at these various stages, although practice may be shifting. It is difficult to define teaching competencies in detail, and hence even more complex to define levels of attainment in learning to teach. There have been attempts to do this by drawing on models of professional skill acquisition (McClelland 1976), as Edwards and Collison (1996) do. They relate a five-level model to the pre-service training and continuing professional learning of primary teachers. Edwards and Collison suggest that Level 2 (advanced beginner) might be expected at the end of a first school practice and this would mean that the, 'competencies demonstrated by the student might include the following: an ability to vary the management of pupil learning, an ability to use questioning to engage children's learning, an ability to provide resources that support children's learning' (1996:114). At the end of their training students should be at Level 3 (competent), and their abilities here might include, 'an ability to manage the learning of a whole class, an ability to plan teaching sessions for the learning of children across the ability range, an ability to work effectively with other teachers in long-term curriculum planning' (1996:114).

What such a model tries to offer is a way of breaking down some of the complexities of skilful practice. Another possibility is to make a distinction between 'learning about' and 'competence in' (Benton 1990; Allsop and Benson 1997). Thus the first assessment may be primarily concerned with progress towards competence rather than observable achievement of the desired competence. Another option, associated with modular approaches to learning to teach, is to select certain competencies as more appropriate for earlier assessment, and others for later (Moon and Shelton-Mayes 1995; Haggarty 1996). Thus competencies that are concerned with teacher knowledge or teaching skills might be the focus for earlier assessment, whereas those concerned with the nature and quality of pupil learning might be the focus of later assessment. In these cases, those students who failed to demonstrate the initial competencies would be required to retake elements of their initial placement, but could not be awarded qualified teacher status until all the competencies, including higher levels ones, had been demonstrated. A further option may be to work with a common set of requirements throughout, but expect different levels of skill in achieving these at different points of the year.

In spite of their differences, all these approaches to interim assessment share a concern to consider explicitly the notion of progression in professional learning. As yet, we know too little about the nature of learning to teach, and in particular about learning to teach in particular subject areas, to reject some approaches and commend others; it may be that future research will enable us to do so. However, there are a number of conclusions that follow. The first is that whatever interim assessment is provided or required does need to be grounded in an explicit model of progression: stage models of professional learning such as that outlined by Edwards and Collison (1996) or modular approaches may be deployed, but some approach to filtering complexity and planning for progression is essential. The second is specific to learning within a subject area. It is unlikely that student teachers will be able to address simultaneously issues related to classroom management and pupil learning early in their training. Our own experience, in three programmes of teacher education, is that issues related to pupil learning and progression are qualitatively different from issues related to classroom organization and management and effective assessment practices will allow and acknowledge the extent to which students have mastered teaching issues before moving on to learning related issues.

Principles

As with observation and discussion, there are a series of principles that
research and experience suggest should underpin effective assessment
approaches (McIntyre and Hagger 1993).

The first of these is that those who are most knowledgeable about
the student's achievements are those who should be the key people
involved in the assessment of the student. That means that the staff
who routinely work with the student, in normal and everyday circumstances, are best placed to comment authoritatively on the student's level of achievement, whether it is an interim assessment, or
a decision related to the award of QTS. The student's mentor will be
the most knowledgeable, and to ensure that all those staff working
with the student contribute to the assessment decision, the mentor
will play an important role in drawing together all the information
gained through formative assessment, to ensure that the summative
judgement is based on a wide range of evidence. Although those
working with the student on a day-to-day basis will be most knowledgeable about the sorts of things that the student can achieve, it
may be that they are less knowledgeable about the standards they
should reasonably expect of a beginning teacher. As Edwards and
Collison (1996) indicate, assessments of students are, in part, criterion referenced. Consider, for example, the requirement that
the student, 'ensure that pupils acquire and consolidate knowledge,
skills and understanding in the subject' (DfEE 1997a:2m). Although
the particular school staff involved can be confident that the student
can achieve that standard or criterion, they may be less sure that
the student does it well enough; there is also a norm referenced
element to this judgement. Thus in making the judgement it may
be necessary for those most knowledgeable about an *individual's*
achievements to have access to those who are more knowledgeable
about what *generally* can be expected of beginning teachers.

Ensuring that the judgement arrived at by the mentor is accurate
and fair is a key issue in assessment. The collection, over time, of a
range of different types of evidence relating to all the assessment
criteria is an essential element in the validity and reliability of judgements. 'The act of assessment is not so much a question of watching
a student looking for competence. Competence is more a matter of
general capability observed over time and in different situations'
(Edwards and Collison 1996:115). Probably the least reliable type of
assessment entails a single assessor basing a judgement on a single,
brief assessment event (Satterly 1989). Thus validity and reliability
can be enhanced, for example, by collecting classroom observation

reports from several staff, thus avoiding the danger of idiosyncrasy, from observations of all the student's classes and at different times in the placement. To these can be added other sorts of evidence: notes of planning meetings and evidence of the student's engagement in parent consultation evenings, of contributions to departmental meetings and of written assignments. The type of evidence required will, in part, be determined by the nature of the criteria, and since a dominant concern is the student's professional competence, class-room observation evidence will be a key source for the judgements. Even with clear assessment criteria and a substantial body of evid-ence on which to base the judgement, interpretation is bound to play a part when something as complex as teaching competence is being assessed. If the criteria for assessment were formulated so simply as to ensure that there was no element of interpretation involved then the consequence would almost certainly be that validity had been sacrificed for reliability (Edwards and Collison 1996) and that what was being assessed bore little relation to the complexities of teaching.

The judgements made, based on multiple sources of evidence will have to be recorded and reported. The nature of the record and form of the report required will vary depending on specific course circumstances and whether or not it is an interim or final judge-ment, but there are common characteristics that all such records and reports should share. They should normally be open to the student and all those working with him or her. There is no sound argument for excluding the student from this knowledge, although we under-stand that it is not unusual for this to be the case. The student is engaged in professional activity; interim summative judgements should form the basis for future development plans and the student is far more likely to understand and engage in these if he or she understands their foundation. Where final judgements are concerned it seems difficult to justify why adults should not be fully informed about a decision that determines their future. Similarly, judgements should be honest. There is clearly a significant tension between this and the need to encourage and support the student, but this tension is not resolved by being dishonest with the learner about progress and achievements. Any recorded or reported judgement should be backed up by evidence, and the inclusion of specific evidence to support specific judgements make openness and honesty more of a possibility. It is far harder to be open when the judgement is based on no more than a hunch, opinion or prejudice and it is difficult to be honest when there is nothing to support the assessment offered.

These principles are not always easy to enact. There *are* tensions between the mentor's role as supporter and assessor, as counsellor and judge. One of the least attractive elements in being a mentor is precisely this tension between acting as guiding hand and final arbiter. Adopting the dual roles is a necessary requirement of the job, unless the task of assessment is to be transferred to those who are less knowledgeable about the student, and in this case, the evidence is that more would be lost than gained. It creates tensions which are recorded in most writing about mentoring (Williams 1993; Furlong and Maynard 1995; Brooks and Sikes 1997; Cameron-Jones and O'Hara 1997): many mentors are acutely aware of it and so too are student teachers. The duality is not unique to mentoring; most teachers, whoever they teach, are also involved in the assessment of the learners. In history, as in other subjects, the tension is exacerbated at GCSE by the existence of coursework assignments. But it takes on a distinctive character when the teacher works with the learner on an individual basis, from day-to-day, over an extended period of time, and in an enterprise that requires such a strong personal commitment. There cannot be any easy way to resolve the tension, but its negative effects can be lessened by trying to ensure that the relationship between mentor and student is, first and foremost, a professional one, rather than a personal friendship; that the focus for their work together is on developing the skills and abilities of learning to teach, rather than, for example, changing one's personality; and that their conversations about progress and achievements relate to publicly agreed and shared criteria about professional competence, rather than personal preferences. Furthermore, tensions are likely to be exacerbated where information about a student's progress is, so to speak, 'locked' away in the mentor's individual discharge of responsibility: others in the school and the department have roles to play, and the more the mentor is playing a coordinating and directing role, drawing on the expertise of others in the school, the less likely it is that tensions that emerge will be focused on the mentor–student relationship.

Any tension that exists in the dual roles is likely to be most acute if the student is judged, at whatever stage, to be failing in some way. In this situation mentors may well experience a sense of personal failure – that they have let down the student and that had they been a better mentor the student would have succeeded. For some mentors the issue may become a confused one about who it is who is failing: student or mentor. It seems too that this feeling of personal failure on the part of mentors is much more acute in this context that when, say, one of their GCSE pupils gets an E grade or an A-level student an F grade. This is partly for the same reasons as the tension between supporter and assessor and also perhaps because in the teaching of school pupils it is easier to accept the range of factors that affect success, of which quality of teaching is only one. In the relatively intense relationship between student and mentor it is easy to see the quality of mentoring as the only significant factor. To some extent, questions about the quality of mentoring in this situation are legitimate. Did the student receive appropriate support and opportunities? If they did not, is there a case for extending the student's experience, perhaps in a new context? Are the judgements that have been made legitimate, and do they fulfil the requirements we indicated earlier in terms of validity and reliability? If the answers to these questions are yes, then the judgements should stand, however tough these are to make. It would clearly be professionally irresponsible – to the student, to any school who employs them and to pupils they may teach – to declare a new teacher competent when they are not.

The final issue of principle concerns the role that the students themselves play in the assessment process. We have already indicated that we believe that they should be fully aware of the judgements being made about them. To what extent should they actually contribute to these judgements? The introduction of various forms of profiling in ITE has, in part, been a response to this issue and the case studies reported in the collection edited by Hustler and McIntyre (1996) indicate the sorts of issues and dilemmas that various institutions and their partner schools have wrestled with in determining an appropriate role for the student. Those studies suggest that there is great value, especially in terms of the students' learning, in their full involvement in discussing and making judgements about progress and achievements. However, full involvement does not necessarily mean that the final judgements are actually negotiated; such a negotiation is likely to be an abdication of responsibility by the mentor and other staff or tutors involved. Although we would hope that all such decisions could be agreed by all parties involved – and if there is disagreement amongst the staff involved external advice should be sought – it should not be the student's view that prevails. The gatekeepers to the profession should be those inside, and not those outside.

Procedures

Specific assessment procedures will be determined by particular courses, and many different versions are possible, although we believe that the sorts of principles we have outlined above should inform any particular sets of arrangements. To illustrate how these principles might eventuate in practice we have chosen two case studies of history students: one a 'failing' student who eventually withdraws from her course; the other a success. We have only included the school-based elements of assessment. We offer no commentary on these cases; they speak for themselves of the difficulties and demands of assessment.

Case study 1: Sarah

Sarah Gardiner was 32 when she began her Postgraduate Certificate of Education (PGCE) course. After graduating with a history degree she spent a year travelling before gaining a Teaching English as a Foreign Language (TEFL) qualification and was then employed in a series of posts teaching English, mainly to adults. She had also been employed as a nursing auxiliary, working with elderly people. Her PGCE year was organized so that after a three week placement in one school she would then spend from mid-October to May attached to another school, returning to her first school for the final four weeks of the year. In her first, short-school placement, designed to be an orientation experience and involving mostly observation and general helping out, all went well and the brief, unstructured report from the school stated that she was keen to learn, asked a lot of questions and was always quick to work and talk with individual pupils.

From mid-October until December she spent two days a week in school, and had a designated mentor, Tania, responsible for organizing and directing her programme. She worked with classes in the variety of ways we have described earlier: observing her mentor and other teachers, working collaboratively with them, and teaching – initially with only limited responsibility for parts of lessons or groups of pupils. Her timetable of contact with classes was varied from week to week to give her a range of experience, although there were two classes that she worked with regularly so that she would also have continuity of experience. The school had very clear schemes of work and, as there were several non-specialists teaching history, for many lessons suggested lesson plans were also available. Sarah tended to use these to guide her own teaching, which seemed reasonable at this stage in her development. She continued to seem keen to learn, and it was clear that she was very good at working with individuals – increasingly pupils in classes would actually ask for Miss Gardiner on the days when she wasn't there. Tania was conscious that when they worked collaboratively together Sarah was keen to avoid introducing lessons but with help in planning would take a leading role further into the lesson. In mid-November her university tutor visited the school and discussions between the tutor and mentor resulted in both agreeing that together they should encourage Sarah to take more responsibility for the lessons in which she was involved. In addition they had both been struck by the fact that Sarah sometimes came across as very muddled in explanations that she gave, and they agreed that this lack of clarity might indicate both muddled thinking and a lack of confidence, possibly causes of concern. Two weeks later, towards the end of the first term, the first formal report on Sarah's progress was due. This required mentor, student and tutor to indicate, in relation to three broad categories of competence (classroom teaching, thinking about teaching including planning and evaluation, and general professional qualities) if progress was satisfactory, a cause for concern or unsatisfactory. The procedures emphasized that progress should be assessed in terms of the student's learning about these issues, not in terms of her competence to achieve all that was specified. Given that stipulation, mentor, tutor and Sarah agreed that progress was satisfactory, although they made it clear to Sarah that in relation to specific criteria within the categories, for example, relating appropriately to whole classes, she needed to make a lot of progress.

From January, Sarah was full time in school and within a fortnight concerns were beginning to emerge. She was now working regularly with seven classes (two from Years 7 and 9, a Year 8, Year 10 and Year 12) and three members of staff in addition to her mentor. Each of these staff was expected to observe at least one lesson for each class once a fortnight, and pass copies of their observation reports to both Sarah and Tania. From these Tania, could see that although staff were trying to be very positive with Sarah two themes seemed to be recurring: that she was too dependent on the member of staff for ideas for her lessons and that her expectations of pupils both in terms of behaviour and standard of work were too low. There were frequent comments such as, 'If you've asked for quiet for an activity, insist on it and take action if you don't get it. Use the referral system', or 'It was clear that the pupils could all do what you'd asked – good instructions. But do you think some found it too easy?' In her own discussions with Sarah, Tania had found herself increasingly irritated by Sarah's poor organization: she never seemed to have the right things with her or to be quite sure where she was going next. When she discussed the observation reports with Sarah, Sarah was very open that she found it difficult to think of ideas for lessons, and that anyway it seemed a bit 'silly to keep re-inventing the wheel'. She was not aware that her lessons were underestimating pupil abilities. It seemed to Tania that Sarah was unaware of what pupils could be capable of achieving in history. Although Tania had been open with Sarah, and had made it clear that there were real concerns over her progress, Sarah did not seem particularly worried: her view seemed to be that she was a beginner and that she was doing well enough.

Tania's concerns grew. She rarely left Sarah alone with her own Year 9 group as she was very worried that mayhem would follow. Members of the Year 12 group had been to see their 'normal' teacher saying that they were concerned that she didn't make things clear to them: they had exams after Easter. Tania knew that things were better with Year 7 and that the teacher who worked alongside Sarah with Year 8 had faith that Sarah could improve. She decided, in consultation with the university tutor, that the time had come to adjust Sarah's programme to give her a better chance of making significant progress. Having discussed it with her colleagues, mentor, student and tutor talked through the new timetable. It involved reverting to collaborative and support teaching with Year 12, dropping the difficult Year 9 class and support teaching with one of the Year 7 groups. With the remaining classes, there were to be clear targets for Sarah. At every point Tania tried to relate these to the assessment criteria: with the Year 7 class Sarah was to focus on her own ideas for lessons – one of the planning criteria as well as being linked to general professional qualities; with Year 9, making her expectations of behaviour clear and enforcing these; with Year 10, raising her expectations of pupil achievement. With Year 8, no specific target was set, with the implication that she was already doing reasonably well with this group. They agreed that progress would be formally reviewed in three weeks time, prior to the submission of the second formal report on Sarah's progress.

With the lightened load there was a slight improvement in Sarah's performance. Observation reports on Year 9 commented that 'you got them really quiet for the register – good', 'good, you split that disruptive pair, and you did it quietly and efficiently', and a Year 7 report stated 'excellent choice of the activities suggested for the lesson on Elizabeth – I think you picked the most appropriate'. But the worrying signs were still very evident. With Year 9, 'Don't run out of steam and let them get away with things at the end of the lesson. When it's break you can always keep them behind as a form of punishment.' With Year 10, there were questions raised about the pace of the lesson; 'Set them time limits, expect more of them.' With Tania's own Year 7 group, comments such as the following appeared. 'I'm not sure you'd really thought through the activity, beyond what's in the departmental handbook. If you did it again what instructions would you give about how to fill in the chart? Would it have been better to divide up the sources between them?' On another occasion, 'Your recap questions at the beginning were really good – clear and focused. But what about the ones after the task – how did those take their thinking forward?' There were no signs of improvement in the Year 10 class and the teacher responsible was becoming increasingly concerned. The pupils were behaving themselves but he felt they were learning little. Sarah herself was looking exhausted and dispirited, and Tania found it hard to know what was best in their meetings: whether to focus on what was being achieved or on the weak areas needing improvement.

When the time came for constructing the second formal report, Tania drew on all the observation reports she had, in addition to her own knowledge of working with Sarah to draft the following report (Table 5.1).

Tania circulated this to colleagues to ask for anything further they would like to add and also asked them to consider whether Sarah could make the progress needed in the remaining six weeks in school after Easter. The responses she received suggested considerable doubt; her own view was that it was very doubtful.

All this was discussed with the tutor, and Tania and she agreed that in their view Sarah's interests would be best served by withdrawing from the course. However, there was enough hope expressed by colleagues to legitimate her staying on if she were determined to continue. The three of them met and Sarah was shown the report. Sarah's reaction was one of surprise, not so much at individual comments but that the whole package represented a cause for such serious concern. She admitted that she was having doubts about teaching, which was much harder work and less enjoyable than she had anticipated. None the less, she was reluctant to give up, partly because she was not convinced that the problems were as extensive as her mentor and tutor thought and partly because the course was now two-thirds complete. Tania and her tutor tried to persuade her to withdraw from the course. They argued that the difficulties Sarah was having seemed to have a common theme to do with her reluctance to 'take control' – of planning, of learning, of behaviour – and to 'be the teacher' with all that involves in mainstream schools. Sarah was adamant that she should continue, and understood that two weeks after Easter her timetable would have to be increased as it was currently too light a load to be regarded as a reasonable basis for final judgements at the end of her practice, a month later.

Table 5.1   Assessment, case study 1

Assessment criteria: areas of concern	Comment
Teaching qualities 1.8 Help pupils understand the subject matter of the lesson 1.11 Ensure that the pupils are making progress 1.12 Monitor pupils' progress 1.13 Ensure that pupils are aware of their progress	Although Sarah may achieve all of these in the context of an individual lesson, for a particular class, she has yet to achieve them systematically for a series of lessons. She needs to develop an overall sense of responsibility for the pupils' learning, over a period of time, and what she must do if this is to be achieved.
Qualities of educational thinking 2.1 Take account of a range of factors when planning your lessons (e.g. subject matter) 2.2 Make balanced judgements about your own and other teachers' lessons	*Planning* For individual lessons this needs to take greater account of the pupils' abilities, especially in terms of raising her expectations of them. In addition she needs to think about each lesson in relation to others. *Evaluation* Although Sarah is honest in her evaluations, she is finding it hard to recognize what level of competence is required of her.
Professional qualities 3.1 Collaborate with colleagues on a professional basis 3.4 Manage your own time 3.7 Relate appropriately to: (a) individual pupils; (b) small groups; (c) whole classes	Sarah tends to rely too much – for this stage of the year – on the advice of colleagues. She needs to take more initiative and assume greater responsibility. Sarah is working on time management but finds it very hard to manage her time efficiently. Sarah is still finding it hard to relate appropriately to whole classes. She is excellent with individuals but needs to be more assertive in the classroom so that she can effectively direct and monitor the pupils' learning.

Sarah began the next term much as she had finished the last, feeling exhausted, and with considerable difficulties in many of her lessons. At best she was keeping the pupils occupied while she worked, very well, with individuals, but the early observation reports and discussions with Tania suggested that there was no discernible improvement. Very much to everyone's surprise, at the end of the first week Sarah announced that she was withdrawing from the course. She said that although she still didn't really understand why she wasn't good enough, she had come to accept the judgements being made, and it seemed increasingly unlikely to her that she would pass.

Case study 2: Tom

Tom was 22 when he began his PGCE. He had come straight from university, where he had done a history and politics degree. Throughout most of his undergraduate career at university he had worked with a student volunteer group teaching English to children for whom English was not their first language. He had also spent two vacations working on summer camps for young people. His training year was organized so that his first six-week block placement ran from late October to December and his second block, at a different school, ran for ten weeks, from February to May.

Tom quickly settled in to his first school. He worked with classes in the range of ways described earlier, but the staff were so impressed by his enthusiasm, commitment and rapid progress that within a fortnight he was assuming responsibility for four classes: two Year 7 groups, Year 8 and Year 9, and taking a major role in the collaborative teaching of a Year 10 group. His mentor, Abra, asked staff to use an adapted version of the final assessment report form for their lesson observations, to give copies of these to both her and Tom and to let her know of any difficulties that arose. There were few. It was evident from both the observation reports and Abra's contact with Tom that he was an unusually successful beginner teacher. The only really difficult class seemed to be Year 9 and it was obvious that Tom was finding it hard to accept that he would not be able to use as wide a range of methods with them as he could with other classes. Abra arranged for him to spend time support-teaching in her own Year 9 group, also known to be a difficult group, so that together they could discuss methods for getting the class to listen and show some respect for each other. She was also somewhat concerned that Tom was wearing himself out: he put so much into every lesson that he was quickly becoming exhausted, and she doubted that he could maintain this pace on his second school placement.

At the end of this placement Abra had to complete a formal report form, and she circulated blank copies of the form to all the staff who had been working with Tom. For each of the criteria for assessment a grade was required from the following:

1 very good, with some outstanding features
2 good, with no significant weaknesses
3 adequate but requires significant improvement
4 poor quality OR no evidence yet – please indicate which of these

Although detailed grade descriptors were not provided, the assessment procedures emphasized that this report came at the end of only six weeks of teaching and so it was anticipated that most students would be graded 3 at this stage. Awarding a 4 for poor quality would mean that serious concern was being signalled. In addition staff had to suggest particular areas of strength and those for development. All the staff knew that this form would be sent to Tom's second school; they received forms for students who came to them for second practice.

From these reports, Abra compiled the following report (Table 5.2).

Please identify two or three particular strengths
Tom is incredibly enthusiastic in the classroom – it's clear he really enjoys being with the pupils and he wants them to get really involved in his lessons. He has already used lots of different methods. He always prepares really carefully and spends a lot of time finding interesting materials to use. His marking has been very thorough and he spends a lot of time commenting on the pupils' work.

Please identify two or three areas for development
1 Record keeping: although Tom's marking is very good his mark book is a shambles – he seems to get very bored with what he sees as trivia!
2 Although Tom has used a wide range of resources in his lessons, including video, he has yet to do anything with IT – he has not had the opportunity. He has also not yet written reviews, although he has attended a parents' evening as an observer.
3 Although Tom's discipline has generally been good he has found Year 9 quite troublesome, and finds it hard to achieve what he wants with them. He would be wise to stick more to lower risk strategies while he develops his management skills.

Table 5.2 Assessment, case study 2, school 1

	1	2	3	4
A Subject knowledge				
1 Secure knowledge, concepts and skills in specialist subject	✓			
2 Detailed knowledge and understanding of the national curriculum KS3 and familiarity with GCSE, A-level and other post-16 syllabuses		✓		
3 Understanding of progression from the KS2 programmes of study			✓ (assumes Year 7 haven't done history before – needs to work on this)	
4 Ability to cope with pupils' subject related questions		✓		
B Planning, teaching and classroom management				
1 Plan to achieve progression in learning, taking account of National Curriculum, GCSE and post-16 syllabuses		✓ (but with Year 9 needs to take more account of behaviour)		
2 Select learning objectives, content and teaching methods for lessons, which are appropriate to what is being taught and the age ability, attainment and prior learning of the pupils		✓	✓ (A-level – hasn't taught this yet)	

Table 5.2 (cont'd)

	1	2	3	4
3 Make effective use of information on pupils' attainment and progress		✓		
4 Able to present content clearly and accurately, using appropriate specialist vocabulary and communicate to pupils their enthusiasm for the subject	✓			
5 Know how to make effective use of IT and other resources to improve standards of pupils' learning		✓ (other resources)		✓ (IT: we don't use it this term)
6 Achieve a good standard of discipline and classroom organization and maintain a safe and purposeful environment for learning	✓ (Years 7, 8)		✓ (Year 9)	
7 Teach whole classes well, monitoring and intervening as necessary to ensure sound learning and ensure effective teaching of groups and individuals		✓		
8 Ensure that pupils acquire and consolidate knowledge, skills and understanding of the subject		✓		
9 Plan opportunities to promote pupils' spiritual, moral, social and cultural development				✓ (who does?)

10 Evaluate critically the effectiveness of their own teaching ✓

11 Stimulate pupils' intellectual curiosity and their enthusiasm for the subject ✓

C Assessment, recording and reporting of pupils' progress

1 Assess on a day-to-day basis how well learning objectives have been achieved and use this assessment to adjust their lesson planning and teaching methods ✓

2 Identify the learning needs of pupils, including able pupils and those with special educational needs ✓

3 Assess pupils' work regularly and provide oral and written feedback to help them make progress ✓ (but his record keeping is a mess)

4 Understand the standards required by the National Curriculum, GCSE and post-16 courses and assess pupils against these with guidance from an experienced teacher ✓ (familiar but hasn't done any yet)

5 Familiar with the statutory assessment and reporting requirements and able to prepare and present informative reports to parents ✓ (hasn't had the chance to do this)

Tom's second school received this form several weeks before Tom's induction week and his mentor there, Simon, tried to take it into account in planning Tom's programme. He decided Tom could benefit from working with two groups that would present significant but different management challenges: a Year 7 group, which seemed to have the whole year's worth of troublemakers; and a Year 9 group which included a particularly difficult group of girls. In addition to another Year 7, a keen Year 8 class and a top set Year 10, he added a Year 12 group and a Year 11 bottom set that he would teach collaboratively with Simon. When Tom first visited the school, he discussed the timetable with him and agreed to put the A-level teaching on hold until after Easter, as Tom wanted to prepare for it, and added in support teaching with another Year 10 group. Tom's second placement went as well as his first and Simon was especially pleased to see that he was making headway with both difficult groups. With the Year 7 class, he was quick to respond to the practical suggestions made by Simon about constantly reinforcing classroom rules, and had accepted that time spent on these was not wasted: it was an investment for the future. Year 9 was hard going, but Tom was prepared to use the full range of disciplinary procedures available to him. Simon's only concern was that two of his colleagues, the usual teachers of the Year 8 and other Year 7 group, were tending to leave him to it too much because everything was going so well. When it came to complete the interim report, half way through the placement, he only had full records from the classes of his that Tom took: the difficult Year 7, the difficult Year 9, the Year 10 group and the bottom set Year 11. This interim report (Table 5.3) required a grade for the overall areas being assessed and a comment on each of these.

Following this, Simon asked the Year 7 teacher to work with Tom on using IT in his lessons, as he knew there were some possibilities to exploit IT effectively and that Tom was so competent with this group that this would be an appropriate challenge. It would also involve the teacher rather more in what was going on. He also asked the Year 8 teacher to show him how he organized his mark book and other records, and asked him to monitor this aspect of Tom's practice. Tom continued to develop his teaching, and this is reflected in the final report that was prepared by Simon. This was compiled by him using all the observation reports he had, versions of the report produced by each of the staff working with Tom, and from Tom's own profile. Throughout the year Tom had been required to comment on his own progress in relation to the criteria and specify targets for improvement. The final stage of this profiling had required him to comment on all the criteria, and Table 5.4 shows extracts from this profile.

Table 5.3 Assessment, case study 2, school 2 interim report

	1	2	3	4
A Subject knowledge		✓		

Comment Generally fine. After Easter will start work with A-level group so will find out about that. Coming on well with Year 10 and GCSE. Good at getting pupils to find out answers when he doesn't know – has the confidence to do this. No problems here.

B Planning, teaching and classroom management	✓	✓		

Comment Planning excellent. Has used lots of different teaching methods, both straightforward and adventurous. Have been especially impressed by his source based work with Year 10. Sometimes things get a bit chaotic because the pupils are so excited by what they're doing. Year 9 is a bit of a struggle, but he is persevering with basic discipline. He does get downhearted when the pupils aren't as enthusiastic as he is. He isn't keen on using IT – he needs to.

C Assessment, recording and reporting of pupils' progress		✓		

Comment His marking is really good and he obviously spends ages on it. We've spent time concentrating on how to organize his mark book – it's still a mess. He wrote some excellent reviews for Year 8 and took the lead for their parents' evening.

Tom's final report is shown in Table 5.5.

Tom and Sarah had very different experiences of assessment, but there are common features of their placement reports. In both cases, summative reports, intended to inform decision making and judgements about their work, were clearly based on classroom experiences. Evidence reflected work with pupils in a variety of classes, and there were detailed and consistent attempts to provide learning experiences that would enable judgements to be made at appropriate levels in the light of experiences. None of the mentors saw their role as involving sole responsibility for exercising judgement about the student; all took advice and welcomed comments from other teachers. All used the expertise of their colleagues. In all the schools, the process of assessment was firmly grounded in classroom practice, generated written evidence and was always open. The outcome for Sarah was withdrawal from teaching but the issues with which she was faced were fully aired. Tom was able to enter the teaching profession with a clear sense of his strengths and weaknesses and a series of insights into the sort of history teacher he was capable of becoming.

Table 5.4 Case study 2 – student responses to profile

Requirement	Response
A3 Understanding of progression from the KS2 Programmes of Study	I know I have improved on this, especially in terms of content. But I'm not yet familiar enough with what the key elements might mean at KS2.
B2 Select learning objectives, content and teaching methods for lessons, which are appropriate to what is being taught and the age, ability, attainment and prior learning of the pupils	There are several classes that clearly require differentiation and so I am constantly thinking about how I can adjust for the high and low ability. I don't think you can begin planning before you consider these factors – and behaviour – they are crucial.
B4 Able to present content clearly and accurately, using appropriate specialist vocabulary and communicate to pupils their enthusiasm for the subject	My lesson feedbacks report my enthusiasm and energy in the classroom and I use appropriate language. My questioning is much more focused now and I don't expect them to read my mind.
B11 Stimulate pupils' intellectual curiosity and their enthusiasm for the subject	I have used a variety of strategies: IT (well, a bit), group work, investigative work, independent projects, role-plays and hot seating to stimulate some very good work from all abilities.
C3 Assess pupils' work regularly and provide oral and written feedback to help them make progress	I have been struggling with the administrative side of teaching but have gradually become more organized and have taken books in regularly and ensured that I feedback to them, their parents and other teachers.

Table 5.5 Assessment, case study 2, final report

	1	2	3	4
A Subject knowledge				
1 Secure knowledge, concepts and skills in specialist subject	✓			
2 Detailed knowledge and understanding of the National Curriculum KS3 and familiarity with GCSE, A-level and other post-16 syllabuses	✓			
3 Understanding of progression from the KS2 programmes of study		✓		
4 Ability to cope with pupils' subject-related questions	✓			

Comment Tom has a sound basis of knowledge as evidenced by a good degree. The skills and understanding thus acquired have enabled him to cope with areas of KS3 with which he is unfamiliar. He has shown great facility at being able to process new material and adapting it for whatever age or ability he is teaching. He is familiar with the GCSE SEG Modern World syllabus and with the AEB 673 A-level syllabus.

B Planning, teaching and classroom management				
1 Plan to achieve progression in learning, taking account of National Curriculum, GCSE and post-16 syllabuses	✓			
2 Select learning objectives, content and teaching methods for lessons, which are appropriate to what is being taught and the age, ability, attainment and prior learning of the pupils	✓			

Table 5.5   (*cont'd*)

	1	2	3	4
3 Make effective use of information on pupils' attainment and progress	✓			
4 Able to present content clearly and accurately, using appropriate specialist vocabulary and communicate to pupils their enthusiasm for the subject	✓			
5 Know how to make effective use of IT and other resources to improve standards of pupils' learning	✓ (other resources)	✓ (IT)		
6 Achieve a good standard of discipline and classroom organization and maintain a safe and purposeful environment for learning	✓			
7 Teach whole classes well, monitoring and intervening as necessary to ensure sound learning and ensure effective teaching of groups and individuals	✓			
8 Ensure that pupils acquire and consolidate knowledge, skills and understanding of the subject	✓			

Table 5.5 (*cont'd*)

	1	2	3	4
9 Plan opportunities to promote pupils' spiritual, moral, social and cultural development			✓ (these happen but he doesn't plan for them)	
10 Evaluate critically the effectiveness of their own teaching	✓			
11 Stimulate pupils' intellectual curiosity and their enthusiasm for the subject	✓			

Comment All Tom's lessons are very well planned, taking account of age, ability and behavioural problems. He has been conscientious about finding out as much as he can about his pupils and uses a wide range of different teaching strategies in order to cater for individual needs. His oral input is very clear and enthusiastic. The atmosphere in the classroom is generally orderly and purposeful, although sometimes he finds it hard to contain the enthusiasm he has created. He checks understanding through questioning and written reinforcement. He uses historical issues to promote discussion, asking children to make up their minds on the basis of the evidence. Every lesson is evaluated and he uses the insights thus gained to plan for the future. His classroom management and the nature of the history curriculum mean that moral, social and cultural understanding is developed.

	1	2	3	4
C *Assessment, recording and reporting of pupils' progress*				
1 Assess on a day-to-day basis how well learning objectives have been achieved and use this assessment to adjust their lesson planning and teaching methods	✓			

Table 5.5   *(cont'd)*

	1	2	3	4
2 Identify the learning needs of pupils, including able pupils and those with special educational needs	✓			
3 Assess pupils' work regularly and provide oral and written feedback to help them make progress		✓ (let down by his record keeping)		
4 Understand the standards required by the National Curriculum, GCSE and post-16 courses and can assess pupils against these with guidance from an experienced teacher		✓		
5 Familiar with the statutory assessment and reporting requirements and able to prepare and present informative reports to parents		✓		

Comment   Tom checks understanding regularly and adapts lesson plans as a result. He has gained experience in identifying pupils' needs but is also reliant (as are all teachers) on the records and knowledge of other staff. He is conscientious about marking and his written and oral comments are designed to help pupils progress. Pieces of assessed work are clearly focused on a type of understanding or skill. His records have improved but could still be more organized and systematic. He is familiar with statutory reporting and assessment requirements and has shown competence and perception in both writing reviews and reporting to parents orally about pupils' progress and achievements.

Part Two

INDUCTION

James Arthur and Jon Davison,
edited by Anna Pendry and Chris Husbands

6

THE INDUCTION OF NEWLY QUALIFIED HISTORY TEACHERS

However effective ITE is, there is considerable research and empirical evidence to suggest that the first year of teaching is of considerable significance to the future development of newly qualified teachers (Earley 1993:10). For over 25 years, it has been recognized that although ITE can develop some areas of competence, others 'are better left until they can be built on school experience and personal maturity' (DES 1972:73; see also Alexander *et al.* 1984; Ofsted 1993). It is also clear that the quality of support provided for new teachers during their induction can 'turn them on or turn them off', and 'experiences of the first term [are] likely to colour all subsequent attitudes to teaching' (Draper *et al.* 1992). A series of research reports note what they call 'reality shock': even in school-based and competency-focused programmes of teacher education, the transition from ITE to employment can prove difficult for NQTs (Koestler and Wubbels 1995). They are generally more isolated than during initial training, when they would have a peer group of fellow students in the same school or in the same higher education institutions. Support and advice from higher education based tutors, which was a feature of initial training, is clearly not available during the first year of teaching. Most NQTs will be teaching a more intensive timetable, for a longer period of time, than they taught even at the end of the initial training. And, finally, but significantly, NQTs will be coming to terms in many cases with the personal and social demands created by settling in a new area.

Large scale surveys of induction programmes for NQTs suggest considerable variety in the nature, scope and quality of provision (HMI 1988; Ofsted 1993; Earley and Kinder 1994). Although schools are clearly aware that new teachers face a variety of personal and professional demands when settling into a new school, with distinctive procedures and routines, their responses vary considerably. Some schools allocate NQTs a designated subject mentor, who they are able to see on a regular, timetabled, basis, and who may well observe the NQT's classroom teaching. Such provision, although clearly expensive, recognizes that NQTs need to develop their subject teaching skills in the context of a new school with new demands. Other schools vest responsibility for induction in the hands of the head of department. Although such contacts provide valuable opportunities for NQTs to acquire information about departmental policies, routines and procedures, heads of department are frequently exceptionally busy, and perhaps particularly so early in the school year (Earley 1993). There is some evidence that NQTs find it difficult to explore classroom related issues with those who in other respects are their 'line managers'. Other schools, perhaps more typically, entrust the task of induction to a deputy head, who takes overall responsibility for NQTs and staff development. This strategy recognizes the need to relate NQTs' needs to wider staff and continuing professional development provision in the light of the school's development, but it rests on the implicit assumption that subject related learning has been completed in initial training, and that induction support is more likely to be generic in nature (O'Sullivan *et al.* 1997). Finally, some schools and Local Education Authorities (LEAs) continue to provide opportunities for NQTs from a number of schools to work together, on a half-day release or residential weekend basis. The evidence is that NQTs value these opportunities to establish a local professional 'peer group' and to set their own experiences into context, but they have become less common in recent years and, even at their best, cannot replace the need for effective in-school support.

The range of provision suggests that schools themselves have different ideas about what constitutes effective induction. Schools appear to establish different relationships between: subject-specific and generic support; school-focused and LEA-led support; and the need for new teachers to explore classroom difficulties and the formal management structures of the schools. Equally, newly qualified teachers enter the profession with a wide range of needs, which change extremely quickly in the light of first-term and first-year experiences. To some extent, the development of Career Entry Profiles (Teacher Training Agency 1997) will help to provide a more effective evidential base on which induction can be built. In this chapter we explore the issues surrounding induction: why effective induction might be difficult and practice so variable and the principles that should underpin effective induction. Our concern is with the development of classroom history teaching, so we concentrate on induction in this area. We do not, for example, discuss the needs of NQTs as form tutors, or in relation to whole-school issues. In Chapter 9, we examine what these principles might look like in practice, through a case history of the experience of one newly qualified history teacher.

Why effective induction is difficult

The most recent evidence we have of the state of induction nationally comes from the HMI report, *The New Teacher in School* (Ofsted 1993). That report paints a gloomy picture of very variable practice and concludes that in the five years since they last reviewed such provision there had been only 'marginal improvement' (Ofsted 1993:40). That the White Paper, *Excellence in Schools* (DfEE 1997c), needed to assert the aim of giving 'every new teacher guided support during the first year' (1997c:47), and the Sutherland Report to note the importance of structured arrangements for NQTs (Sutherland 1997), suggests that despite the widespread acceptance of the importance of induction, achieving improvement is proving very difficult.

One of the reasons why induction practices are so variable and effective induction relatively elusive is that it is difficult to be clear about its goal. Unlike ITE, where we can at least state the goal of 'training good teachers' – however complex this turns out to be – there is no simple formulation of a goal for induction. Induction must have multiple goals: the initiation of the NQT into the culture of the specific school (Earley and Kinder 1994; Davison 1997); the development of a professional identity (Calderhead 1992); the consolidation of skills developed in initial training and the development of skills not addressed in ITE (Ofsted 1993); an introduction to the culture of the profession (Earley and Kinder 1994); and the beginning of a career-long process of professional growth (Steffy 1989). This range of goals reveals two important tensions. One concerns how the NQT is viewed; as a competent teacher or as a learner (Carney and Hagger 1996). The other concerns the desired outcome of induction; helping the NQT to fit in or to be capable of contributing to change. These tensions cannot easily be resolved since the NQT has to be *both* teacher and learner and induction has to have *both* a normative, conservative function and yet also have a dynamic to ensure that new teachers have the potential to contribute to the development of pedagogy (Calderhead 1992).

A second reason why induction poses difficulties is that although it is widely recognized as a phase in teacher development, a process begun in ITE and continuing long into teachers' careers, the knowledge that we have about the nature of this phase and its connections with ITE is comparatively superficial. The models of teacher learning that we outlined in Chapter 2 (pp. 30–2) are all drawn from studies of student teachers, and those we draw on in Chapters 8 and 9 (on the continued professional development of history teachers) tend to say little about the connections between initial learning and professional development in the first few years of teaching. Although the need to provide effective relationships between initial training and induction is generally acknowledged (Earley 1993:5), research into the processes of learning to teach has tended to end with the award of qualified teacher status. There have been few longitudinal studies in the UK that explore new teachers' experiences in their first years of teaching. In addition, the studies that have concentrated on the first years of teaching (e.g. Earley and Kinder 1994; Tickle 1994) were conducted prior to the recent massive changes to ITE, which means that we should interpret their findings with care.

Our lack of knowledge about the nature of NQTs' professional learning has been compounded by the absence of mechanisms to assist in linking ITE with the first year of teaching. The Ofsted report, *The New Teacher in School* (1993), reported that many headteachers were unaware of the kind of training their NQTs had received prior to taking up their posts, and that schools tended to be relatively ignorant of the new teachers' strengths and weaknesses. In many cases it is likely that the only direct communication between training institution and employing school has been the reference, a document designed to support an application and not to provide any substantial picture of future development needs. In the mid-1990s Earley reported that many headteachers and LEA officers felt that structural changes in education were making it more, rather than less difficult to establish closer links between ITT institutions, LEAs and schools in relation to induction (Earley 1993:6).

The diversity of new teachers' needs, especially in relation to the resources available in schools, is another reason why effective induction is so demanding. Again, the evidence that we have of the nature of these needs predates recent changes in ITE and so it may be that at least some of these are shifting in character. In 1992, Calderhead, acknowledging that the increased level of school-based work may mean that terms such as 'culture shock' might no longer be appropriate, none the less argued that there were persistent areas of difficulty commonly experienced by new teachers, and that knowledge of these should inform the design of induction systems. The four areas he identified are: classroom skills; curriculum and planning; adapting to the workplace and school culture; and the personal/professional dimension (Calderhead 1992).

The first of these, classroom skills, included discipline, classroom management, motivating pupils and catering for a wide range of abilities (Calderhead 1992:8). Ofsted (1993) similarly identified three areas concerned with catering for diverse pupil needs: differentiation; the teaching of pupils with special education needs; and the teaching of English as a second language. They also identified aspects of assessment as an area of difficulty for NQTs. It seems entirely reasonable that all of these should still be areas of difficulty for NQTs, whatever the changes in ITE, since these are some of the most significant challenges in teaching reported by the annual report of Her Majesty's Chief Inspector (HMCI) (Ofsted 1997b). Where management and discipline are concerned the tasks facing new teachers are extremely complex. As Calderhead comments, 'even experienced teachers, when asked how long it took them to become competent in various areas of classroom teaching, have estimated that basic managerial skills have taken at least five years to master' (Calderhead 1992:9). The same conclusion applies to classroom skills more directly related to pupil learning and pupil needs. In Section 1 we saw that it is not until some way into their training that student teachers can begin seriously to consider these issues, and the need for greater differentiation and the development of assessment practices have been frequent comments in Ofsted reports on experienced history teachers' practice (Ofsted 1994, 1996). In referring to these difficulties for NQTs, HMI prefaced their comment with the statement that 'there are some skills which, for most students, are unlikely to be developed within their initial training and should receive specific attention during the period of induction' (Ofsted 1993:36). The complexity of this aspect of practice and a recognition of the limits of ITE, make it reasonable to suppose that they will represent continuing areas of difficulty for NQTs, in which they will need considerable support.

Calderhead (1992) identifies the second area of difficulty as curriculum and planning. Here he is referring to familiarity with subject matter and the development of techniques for transforming this into learning activities in the classroom. It may be that in certain respects this represents less of a difficulty now that the national curriculum has reduced variability in school history curricula. NQTs will be familiar with many of the study units and with a wide range of teaching and learning strategies. Even if this is the case, as Ofsted suggests (Ofsted 1997b) the process of transforming subject matter to make it accessible and interesting is so complex, involving so many kinds of teacher knowledge, that it will always be an aspect of practice that can be developed and improved, especially as NQTs become more knowledgeable about learners. In addition there will be many areas where they do not have prior knowledge of subject matter, especially in GCSE syllabuses for Key Stage 4, and A-level syllabuses where practice is more variable. We therefore suggest that although this may be less of a difficulty than in the past it is certainly still an area of need, and lesson planning remains a time consuming activity for beginners (Davison 1997).

Adapting to the workplace and the school culture is the third area of difficulty identified by Calderhead (1992). Although it seems likely that much more time spent in school in training and much greater involvement in the life of the school will have alerted NQTs to the culture of schooling, the process of adaptation will still be difficult because all schools are distinctive. It may be here that the tension over NQT as teacher and NQT as learner is most acute. To gain acceptance as a colleague an NQT will want to present himself or herself as fully competent, and in acknowledging him or her as a colleague the school will view the NQT as a fully competent professional who needs time and space to consolidate his or her practice (Carney and Hagger 1996). However, NQTs may also be very aware of the need to continue to learn and for support and the challenge to do so, and this may well conflict with what they perceive as the expectations for them, and indeed with their own aspirations.

The final area of difficulty identified by Calderhead is the personal/professional dimension. For many new teachers, classroom and professional issues are closely related to their own sense of personal identity and self-esteem. Difficulties or initial failures as a teacher are therefore frequently construed by NQTs as personal failures. In addition, there are more mundane personal issues such as, for example, accommodation, isolation in a new part of the country, and reconciliation of the demands of family with work. These practical needs are also ones that have to be addressed in designing a programme of induction, even though these may seem to have little direct relevance to the NQT's teaching of history. Given the diversity of NQTs' needs it is not surprising that effective programmes are extraordinarily difficult to construct and implement.

The allocation of inadequate resources to induction in some schools is the final issue we raise in discussing the challenges of induction. In many cases it seems that responsibility for induction in subject teaching is subsumed within existing job descriptions and that the head of the history department, for example, will take on the role of inducting a new colleague with no specific allocation of time and no specific training offered (Bush *et al.* 1996). Even where the intention is to adopt more formal procedures and provision this may mean little in practice. A teacher quoted by Bush made precisely this point: 'There's a lot of talk about mentoring [NQTs] but nothing had actually been set up. There's all these good intentions but nothing has been followed through' (Bush *et al.* 1996:129). In some respects it may be appropriate to compare the current situation in induction with that of ITE some time ago. Before the recent changes in ITT, it was very common for schoolteachers to act as subject supervisors to student teachers with no time allowance and a comparatively limited view of their role with students: lending classes and providing practical suggestions. Increasingly, those working with students have been designated as mentors, have had this recognized as a distinctive aspect of their work, with some time allowed for it, and have developed their thinking and their practices so that they are making a substantial contribution to a planned programme of initial teacher learning. A similar shift is needed for those with responsibility for the induction of NQTs.

This analysis of the difficulties inherent in providing effective induction may seem depressing, but a recognition of these realities enables us to formulate six principles, which underpin effective induction. These principles owe much to the work that Earley and Kinder (1994) have done in identifying the characteristics of good practice.

Principles of effective induction

The first of these is that NQTs need to be viewed as *learners*, by themselves and by others. If they are merely seen as fully competent teachers then the primary goal for induction will inevitably be their socialization into the culture of the school and opportunities for their development, and the development of the department and school, will be severely limited. They are not learners in the same sense as they were as student teachers. They are now colleagues, qualified teachers, with a wide range of skills and abilities as teachers and significant responsibilities as full members of staff. Understanding them as professionals who have a great deal to contribute to their pupils' learning in history, to the history department and to the school as a whole, but who are also in the early stages of their professional development, will be of benefit not just to them but to all those with whom they work, now and in the future.

A second principle, implied by the first, is that their learning should be guided by the principle of *progression*, from initial teacher education and into the first year of teaching. It may be that the creation of the Career Entry Profile (DfEE 1997a) will prove helpful in this respect, at least in the early stages of transition. The initial identification of areas of individual strength and areas most in need of development, is at least a start in identifying particular professional needs as NQTs begin to work, although it may be also that the particular challenges of the school mean that they have needs that were not apparent in prior experience. We can also assume that these needs will change over the year, as do those of student teachers, and that support later in the year may well be focused on different needs. There is some evidence (Earley and Kinder 1994) that the first term may be characterized by a focus on survival (management issues and fitting in), the second by an increasing concern with teaching and learning issues such as differentiation and assessment, and the third term then sees a shift towards career development and the NQTs' wider contribution to the school. We do not know enough to be confident of the validity of these phases, and it is likely that they will vary between individuals, but they none the less alert us to what might be broad patterns of progression over the first year.

An implication of ensuring that the principle of progression in induction practices is met, is that induction needs to be *planned*. If it is essentially reactive and sporadic it is unlikely to meet the changing needs of the NQTs, nor is it likely to make use of strategies such as regular meetings with a mentor, the observation of the NQT's classroom teaching, observation of experienced teachers by the NQT and collaborative teaching and planning, all of which have been shown to be very effective strategies (Calderhead 1992; Earley and Kinder 1994; Turner *et al.* 1997). These strategies, in many respects similar to those used with student teachers but now with different goals, need to be built into a programme of induction. Planning will also ensure coordination of provision, which may draw on the expertise of a subject mentor, a school professional tutor with overall responsibility for induction and development and possibly support offered by the LEA.

If a programme is to be planned and carried through, there has to be a member of staff with *designated responsibility* for it, and time to carry it out. Although it seems most likely that this will be the head of history (Earley and Kinder 1994), there are difficulties in choosing the most appropriate person. NQTs need someone who will be sympathetic to them and the challenges they face, which might suggest a teacher three or four years into the profession, but NQTs also need someone who can offer expertise, be a good role model and with the capacity to effect change on their behalf, which might suggest someone more senior. Whoever does have responsibility needs to be committed to the role and to see value for themselves, in terms of their own professional development or career advancement: it seems to be important that they have a stake in the process of securing effective induction for a new colleague (Earley and Kinder 1994).

Although the programme of induction needs to be planned it also needs to be *negotiated and flexible* so that it can take account of a range of factors: how the individual new teacher learns; what they perceive as their needs at any particular time; the particular strengths of their designated mentor; and the constraints and opportunities afforded by the timetable and school conditions. The diversity of the needs of new teachers, and our knowledge about the idiosyncrasies of learning to teach, both point to the requirement for a programme which is responsive rather than predetermined.

Finally, effective induction must be part of a *whole school commitment* to professional learning and development. Although this is something out of the immediate control of the history department, there is little doubt that effective induction is most likely to be achieved when all staff are well supported and are seen as the school's key resource, in schools that 'value, develop and support the judgement and expertise of all their teachers in the common quest for improvement' (Fullan and Hargreaves 1994:35).

The principles we have espoused are demanding, but we are conscious of the similarity between these and the various principles we advocated in our earlier discussion of the mentoring of student teachers. It may well be that extending to induction the increasingly common effective practices developed in ITE offers a real way forward. As Calderhead and Shorrock state, 'The period of induction may well be as important as what typically happens in the preservice preparation . . . The contribution of an able mentor in the first few years of teaching may be as important as during initial training' (1997:207).

7

MENTORING AND HISTORY TEACHER DEVELOPMENT DURING THE FIRST YEAR OF TEACHING

We have highlighted the importance for subsequent teacher development of effective and active induction for NQTs. In particular, we have highlighted the importance of designated staff in an NQT's first school, of identifying the experiences and achievements of the NQT during initial training, of planning a structured and progressive programme of induction and of responding to individual needs as the first year of teaching progresses. In this chapter we unpick some of these principles through a case study of one NQT, Tom, whose successful experiences as a student we traced in Chapter 5. Our case study highlights three themes, which research and experience suggest are especially important in the induction phase of professional development. The first is the *multiplicity of aspects to early professional learning*. Even where highly effective student teachers have experienced high quality programmes of ITE they can still find the early years of their work as a professional complex and sometimes overwhelming, characterized by 'coping' in the face of confusion and difficulties (Huberman 1992:130). Secondly, we consider the importance for NQTs of establishing and developing a *professional identity* that reflects the strengths and weaknesses of their own teaching style and approach and enables them to be both teachers and learners. Thirdly, we explore the role that *active induction and mentoring* by the NQT's appointing school can play in order to build on and broaden an NQT's professional qualities. In exploring these themes, Tom's story is not a straightforward case of 'good practice': it suggests some of the ways in which

NQTs and their employing schools may struggle during the period of induction.

Tom had completed a history and politics degree before taking his PGCE, and as an undergraduate had worked with a student volunteer group teaching English to children for whom English was not their first language. He was keen to find a post in an urban, multicultural comprehensive school and was appointed, in the May of his PGCE year, to the second post for which he applied, as a teacher of history and humanities. The school, in a deprived area of a Midlands city, took most of its pupils from two large council estates and an area of Victorian terraced houses. There were 750 pupils on the school roll, including a small sixth form of 60 students. The intake was skewed towards the bottom end of the ability range and the school's academic results reflected its intake. Examination results had been rising over the past few years, but were well below both the national and LEA averages, with 26 per cent of pupils gaining five A*–C grade GCSEs. Over 18 per cent of pupils were eligible for free school meals. None the less, the school was noted locally for its innovation and commitment to providing educational opportunities for all its pupils. Tom was appointed as the only new teacher that year to the humanities faculty: the school taught a modular humanities course in Year 7 and then history as an individual subject to Years 8 and 9. In Years 10 and 11, history was an option, alongside geography and a humanities course, which was largely intended for less able pupils. There was normally a small A-level group.

At the interview for the post, Tom impressed: he came with excellent references from both his university tutor and his mentor in his second placement school. He stressed his commitment to working with pupils across the ability range, and answered questions on both the National Curriculum and statutory reporting and recording requirements with intelligence and insight. As part of the interview procedure, Tom was required to teach a mini-lesson to a half-group of Year 7 pupils, and provided a lively and imaginative evidence-based lesson on the arrival of the Black Death in England. The panel were unanimous in appointing Tom, and after the interview the head said quietly to the deputy that he felt that Tom's appointment would strengthen the humanities department considerably: 'they need someone of his rigour and intelligence'.

Visiting the school

Tom visited the school for a day in July to find his way around, to meet the department and other staff and to collect information on schemes of work. He brought with him his Career Entry Profile (CEP) to show to the Department and Deputy. Yvette, the deputy who had appointed him, glanced at the CEP before saying that the school preferred to see how things went early on rather than basing any induction provision here on Tom's earlier experiences in very different schools. Yvette, who had responsibility for staff development, said that the school had an informal approach to induction, and that she would see Tom monthly to discuss progress, but that her 'door will always be open if you have a problem. But I think you'll find Sue [the head of humanities, a geographer], very positive and supportive.' Tom was also told by Sue that he would be teaching humanities to Year 7, and A-level sixteenth-century European history to a Year 12 group of five pupils. Tom found the day rather overwhelming: the school had schemes of work for every unit, but the history stock cupboard was somewhat disorganized and Mike, history coordinator within the humanities faculty as well as head of Year 8, had been too busy to provide him with a full set of textbooks. Tom said that he was keen to address one of the issues that had been indicated on his CEP; the use of IT in history. Mike said that he too found IT difficult and was delighted that Tom had an interest in this area. Everyone in the department was friendly, but Tom felt confused by the amount of information he had been given, and slightly uneasy by the prospect of teaching geography – which he hadn't studied since the age of 14 – and A-level sixteenth-century history, which he had never before studied.

The first weeks

Tom's next visit to the school did not take place until the day before term began in September: he had difficulty in finding digs locally. He spent his summer mugging up both National Curriculum geography and, using the A-level syllabus, sixteenth-century European history. His timetable arrived in the post in the middle of August, indicating that he would be teaching one Year 7 group, two Year 8 groups, three Year 9 groups, and one Year 10, Year 11 and Year 12 group. He was also given a Year 7 tutor group. By the beginning of term, Tom had developed his own schemes of work for each of the groups and outline plans for the first half term, together with detailed lesson plans for the first ten days of term. The day before teaching began was a whole-school development day, with the morning taken up in a lengthy staff meeting, then a brief humanities department administrative meeting followed by opportunities for staff to sort out their own teaching rooms. Tom was made to feel welcome during the day, and shared his lunch with Sue and Mike.

The first day of term was extremely hectic. The first two of the six lessons in the day were spent with his new tutor group. Tom was slightly thrown by the experience of having 28 eleven-year-olds, all clearly more apprehensive and confused about their new school than he was, looking to him for expert information on finding their way around the school and on administrative details to do with lockers and games kit. After break he taught his first history lesson to a Year 8 history group, spending roughly half the fifty minutes outlining his own expectations and ways of working before working through a simple time line exercise with them. Before lunch he met his Year 12 A-level group for the first time. He found them all extremely quiet and unresponsive. He had hoped for more enthusiasm from an A-level group, and found himself spending most of the time talking at them rather than with them. In the afternoon he taught two lessons, each to a Year 9 group. Although the historical content was identical – an introduction to the Industrial Revolution through the idea of change – he found the second group much harder work than the first; they were noisy and difficult to settle. By the end of the lesson and the end of the day he felt extremely tired, too much so to reflect in detail on the day or to evaluate any of the lessons. Mike, hurrying through the staff room on the way home, saw Tom drinking a cup of coffee and called, 'Everything OK then, Tom?' before leaving.

The hectic pace of the first day characterized the first week; many new faces, new routines, and new material. By the end of the second week, Tom had seen all his groups at least twice and was beginning to identify some common traits. Rather to his surprise, he enjoyed teaching the geography module to his Year 7 groups, but was disappointed at how long it took the pupils to complete what he thought of as relatively straightforward graphing exercises. The Year 8 groups were going well; he was able to recycle some of the activities he had devised for groups on his placements during training and he felt very much on top of the work. The Year 9 groups were more difficult. Already he had found himself shouting at two of the groups and in each of these felt that he was beginning to have difficulties with particular pupils. The Year 10 group had begun their GCSE course well, but the Year 11 group, which he had inherited from the teacher he had replaced, appeared to have covered relatively little of the syllabus in Year 10 and several had elements of coursework 'missing'. His Year 12 group were hard going: there were now only four of them and they said little, so

Tom was falling back on a very didactic A-level style. On top of this, he was becoming keenly aware that Mike, the only other history specialist, was apparently *always* busy and either unable or unwilling to discuss aspects of history teaching with him.

Difficulties emerge

As the term progressed, these patterns became more firmly established. Tom felt that there were some groups that he was teaching well and deploying imaginative strategies with, whereas there were others, notably two of the Year 9 groups, the Year 11 group and the Year 12 group, that were, at best, frustrating and, at worst, very debilitating. One of the Year 9 groups was becoming particularly troublesome, and in the fourth week of term, Tom felt that he lost control of the class. Three boys had become more and more oppositional, and although Tom had punished them by asking them to complete letters of apology and statements of intent on good behaviour, this strategy was simply not working. The noise level was high and little work was being done. At the end of that week, Yvette, the deputy to whom Tom had passed his CEP, arranged her first induction meeting with Tom. She began it by saying that she was hearing 'very good things' about Tom's work from Sue and Mike. Although Tom didn't share this perception, he had become aware of the wider difficulties that staff felt that the school faced, as a school in a difficult setting with relatively poor results, and he did not want to admit to failure. He thanked Yvette and said that he hoped he was working well. Yvette laughed and said that she wished everyone took that attitude. After a pause, Tom said that he was concerned about one of his Year 9 groups. He did not mention the problems with the other groups, and felt that if he could get on top of his biggest problem then he would be able to sort other things out. Yvette thought for a moment and then replied that the three boys with whom Tom was having problems were notorious through the school, and she said that she would 'look in' during Tom's next lesson with the group.

Although Yvette did come in, her intervention with the group had only a temporary effect, and by half term Tom was feeling very downcast. The problems he had identified early on were not easing. Discipline remained an issue with his Year 9 groups, and he was unable to motivate either his Year 11 group or Year 12 group. More than this, Tom felt isolated and lonely. He did not feel able to articulate his difficulties and he did not feel that the faculty, all of whom were very pleasant to him in the staff room, were particularly interested in addressing them. After the success of his initial training he now felt dispirited and ineffective. Just before half term, Mike asked Tom to go to an LEA in-service day on history and IT in his place, as he didn't 'have the time, or, frankly, the inclination really'. Tom was uncertain about whether, in his first term, he should go, but was flattered to be asked. In fact, the day was a turning point. The opportunity to explore issues related to classroom teaching in history with fellow history teachers was invaluable, and Tom felt himself talking animatedly about the classroom for the first time since term began. At lunchtime he chatted to the LEA's history adviser. She welcomed him to the LEA and asked him if things were going well. After a moment's hesitation, Tom told her that he was having some problems, and went into some details. She said that there was probably little she could do, but she would telephone the school and speak to Yvette, who she knew quite well, and try to arrange a visit if that would be helpful. Feeling rather desperate, Tom agreed, although he had reservations that it might look as if he was 'going behind' the school's back.

The adviser telephoned Yvette two days later and arranged to visit the school immediately after half term. Yvette came to Tom's classroom at lunchtime and asked whether they could speak. It was evident to Tom that she wished he had been more honest with her, but none the less she said that she felt that the school had so far let Tom down: they had been so impressed by him at interview that they had, perhaps, failed to identify either his needs or the extent of his difficulties. She said that in a school like this one facing numerous social and academic difficulties, senior and middle managers tended to be very busy, but that this could neither explain nor excuse the failure to address Tom's needs. Tom was both impressed and relieved by her response and they agreed that Tom would meet Sue, the LEA adviser and herself immediately after half term to agree a more formal induction programme to reflect Tom's evident needs.

Active induction and mentoring

The meeting took place the first week after half term. Yvette began it by referring to the hitherto ignored CEP, which suggested that Tom might need some support in classroom management and in using IT in history. She then asked Tom what else he would want to add to the list now. He said that classroom management was certainly an issue, but that he was also very concerned by different problems with his Year 11 group and his Year 12 group. The four discussed options, and an action plan was agreed. They agreed that the main issues to deal with were the management difficulties with Year 9, and, with Years 11 and 12, finding ways for Tom to adapt his approaches and methods to the needs of pupils in this school. With Year 11, helping them to organize their work and understand the demands of GCSE in the final year were identified and, for Year 12, finding ways of motivating, interesting and involving small groups of students who were comparatively weak A-level candidates. Specifically, they agreed on the following.

- Yvette would observe Tom teaching the Year 9 groups that were difficult and debrief him formally on them, identifying specific strategies and approaches that might be generating the difficulties. She would also arrange a programme of observation for him with other teachers who the school felt were effective with difficult groups.
- Yvette also suggested to Tom that the Year 11 difficulties had roots in the groups' Year 10 experience, and that the school's Key Stage 4 coordinator should work with Tom and the pupils in the group. Together they would identify what could be done about the missing work and to set specific targets for each individual to ensure that they focused on the importance of their GCSE work.
- Yvette then turned to the Year 12 group. She and Sue agreed that there were difficulties in teaching and motivating small, and generally not particularly able, sixth-form groups, but suggested that the school would be prepared to release Tom for two or three afternoons to visit other schools where the adviser felt that good practice had been identified in post-16 teaching.
- Yvette suggested to Tom that Sue and he should meet weekly, on Thursday lunchtimes, to an agenda prepared by Tom the day before, to discuss issues and strategies. She suggested that Sue should take the lead on this so that Tom would still have a 'fall back' position and could come to her if there were issues or concerns that were not addressed by Sue.
- Finally, Yvette proposed that the CEP issue on IT be left 'on hold' until Tom felt that the other issues were addressed, and that the four of them should meet again at the end of term to review progress.

Tom agreed to all this. He felt that the school was now responding to the situation in which he found himself and attempting to devise a series of strategies that would help him to address his difficulties.

It was not to be plain sailing for Tom or the department from this meeting. Yvette's observations, and Tom's observations of other teachers, suggested strategies for dealing with the Year 9 groups and individuals within them that began to improve the situation. However, it takes a long time to turn around difficult groups, and Tom felt that he had a difficult term with both groups. However, by Christmas, he was able to set and collect work for both groups on time, and to manage at least some learning without constantly shouting in lessons with both groups. The Year 11 group were all interviewed individually by Tom and the Key Stage 4 coordinator and individual targets were agreed that would plug the gaps in their coursework by the end of January. Tom visited three other schools in the city to observe and discuss strategies for approaching small A-level groups. Although the individual strategies he discussed were valuable in themselves, perhaps just as valuable were the opportunities to look at effective history departments locally and establish contacts and a network with other history teachers. The weekly meetings with Sue were difficult at first, as she was concerned that she might be treating Tom too much like a student teacher and not enough like a colleague, but gradually they began to develop a routine based on growing mutual respect, and the meetings provided a forum within which Tom could discuss his classroom practice and individual pupils. When the LEA adviser, Yvette, Sue and Tom met to review the induction experience at Christmas, there was consensus that a great deal had been achieved.

The group agreed that Tom had considerable strengths in a humanities faculty where history curriculum development and practice had been static for some time. They also agreed that the second term of the year should mainly focus on consolidating the progress that had already been made but that it would be appropriate for Mike (the history coordinator) to become involved to work with Tom on the creation of Year 9 end of term reviews and reporting to parents. To create time for this, the meetings with Sue were reduced to once a fortnight, with Tom meeting Mike in the other weeks to talk through with him his assessment of Year 9 and the ways in which this would then feed into the final reviews. Although Mike clearly had reservations about accommodating this within his schedule as a head of year he was keen to help, and they all agreed to meet again at the end of the second term.

Second term review meeting

By that time, Tom felt somewhat more positive about his work. Although the Year 9 group with the three particularly difficult boys

was still very demanding, his other Year 9 groups were now working very well, and his Year 11 group had all completed their missing
coursework and were now focused on revision for the GCSE examination. The A-level group was beginning to establish a positive
identity, and although they still tended to be very quiet and Tom
had constantly to think of ways of getting them involved in their
work, he felt that he was making some progress with them and at
least beginning to achieve what he wanted. The work on assessment with Mike had definitely helped Tom to extend his understanding of the range of approaches he could use to assess Year 9,
and together they had begun to develop a new recording system for
history. They hadn't succeeded in meeting at all the times intended,
but Tom had felt that as well as learning more about assessment he
had made some sort of contribution to the faculty. At this review
meeting, the LEA adviser resurrected the point about IT in history
made in the CEP. She suggested that Tom might now like to join
termly meetings she hosted looking at an LEA project on CD-ROM
as a classroom resource in history.

Reflections

The experiences of Tom as an NQT prompt some reflections on both
the process of becoming a history teacher and on mentoring NQTs.
Tom was an excellent student teacher who left his training with
real strengths. However, he found it difficult to transfer his skills to
a new setting and experienced some familiar emotions; he felt overloaded, isolated and overwhelmed. When things began to go wrong,
he did not feel able to share his difficulties with colleagues, so that
the difficulties spiralled and by half term Tom was beginning to encounter serious failure. He faced *different* difficulties with different
groups, and in order to address these varied difficulties the school
needed to make a planned institutional and management response.
The school made some disastrous early mistakes. They saw Tom as
a high quality NQT, but in doing so failed to identify that he had
continued learning needs. They failed to use the evidence that was
available, and failed to organize an effective induction programme.
The fact that everyone was generally approachable and supportive
was not enough. The history coordinator, mostly through being
overloaded, was unable to support Tom properly, and although this
was recognized later on, it was not allowed for earlier in the term.
    That noted, once Tom had indicated his difficulties to the LEA
adviser, she was able to prompt the school into action, and the

deputy's positive response to this enabled the school to formulate a plan based on some excellent principles of procedure. This plan used the CEP as only one starting point to identify needs, and encouraged Tom to indicate his needs in this school clearly. A programme of meetings was established, for which Tom, as a fully qualified professional, was allowed to set the agenda. A framework was established with a 'fail-safe' (the opportunity to take difficulties to Yvette) should further difficulties be encountered. The induction programme set in place at half term recognized Tom's expertise, but also saw the need to draw in particular staff for particular issues: the Key Stage 4 coordinator; other staff within the school; and other history A-level teachers locally. One of the issues in Tom's CEP was sensibly left until other, more pressing issues, had been addressed, but the IT issue was not neglected and a strategy was established to address this in the third term.

Although the school made serious, if not untypical, errors in the way they treated Tom early in the year, their actions after half term were planned and effective. They demonstrate the differences between the support that beginning *student* teachers require, and that *newly qualified* teachers require. In the latter case, there is none of the tension between support and assessment that characterizes the former, but there is the need to establish clear institutional frameworks with provision being the responsibility of the school as much as a responsibility of the individual. Moreover, although the cost of the meetings with first Sue and then Mike too, the observation and the involvement of the Key Stage 4 coordinator was not inconsiderable, it is also clear that for the school this was an investment well made. Planned and effective support can turn potential failure into success and help the first year in teaching to be not just a time of coping with crises and fitting in, but a positive phase of teacher development and professional learning.

Part Three

CONTINUED PROFESSIONAL DEVELOPMENT

Chris Husbands and Anna Pendry

8

CONTINUED PROFESSIONAL
DEVELOPMENT: OPPORTUNITIES
AND CONSTRAINTS

Three examples of professional learning

At the end of a school day, three members of the history department who share Year 7 teaching sit around the pupils' tables. Their
task is to re-plan the department's unit on the Roman Empire. They
have two aims: to cover the material in less time, and, more importantly, to redevelop the topic as an introduction to secondary school
history for Year 7 using a number of lively activities that focus on
the nature of the discipline. They begin by working out, in general
terms, the objectives and outline of the unit. They recall activities
that have been used in the past and the pupils' responses to them.
They discuss the importance of pupil enjoyment compared to clear
learning outcomes and there is no clear consensus on this. Each de-
scribes in detail approaches they have used and gradually they build
up a bank of ideas that draws on everyone's suggestions. Some of
the ideas take the team down blind alleys; apparently good ideas
would be too time consuming or make too many resource demands.
Eventually agreement is reached on details of the unit and the team
share out the planning and organizational tasks that now need to
be done. The meeting closes and the three decide to go for a drink.

It is a formal departmental meeting near the beginning of the
school year. The head of department has prepared a paper that
present figures on the number of pupils opting to take GCSE history
over the previous five years and their results. The figures do not
make encouraging reading: there has been a steady decline in the
proportion of the Year 9 cohort opting to study history and the
examination results suggest that history is becoming less attractive

to the most able pupils. There is a discussion about possible causes. These include a feeling that pupils see history as more difficult than other subjects, that changes to the options structure have discriminated against the subject and that the material the National Curriculum obliges them to teach in Year 9 is dull. The head of department recognizes all these, but does not know which, as a department, they should prioritize. After some time, he makes the suggestion that he had prepared and cleared with the headteacher beforehand: that the department should invite the LEA history adviser to tell them about trends and practices elsewhere and make suggestions on how to prioritize.

It is the middle of the school day in a challenging urban comprehensive school. Pupils are moving between lessons, and the head of history watches Year 9 groups come into the history teaching area. One group, waiting outside a classroom for their teacher to arrive, begins to become noisy and jostling starts. Immediately the head of history moves towards them and bellows at them to stand quietly. There is silence. The class's teacher arrives and allows the group into the room to begin their lesson. A Year 10 pupil arrives late for his lesson. The head of department stops him and asks him why he is late. Satisfied with his explanation, the teacher allows the pupil to enter the Year 10 lesson. Some time later, while working in the departmental office, the head of history hears loud and persistent noise from the Year 9 group. She watches the class through the glass panel. The noise level is high and one pupil is seen to throw something across the room. The head of department enters the room and speaks to the class teacher quickly – she says she will take the pupil she has seen throwing something out of the lesson if that would help. The class teacher accepts her offer and tells the pupil to go with the head of department. Noise levels fall and the Year 9 class is able to resume working.

Professional learning in history departments

These three snapshots illustrate three rather different versions of professional development and opportunities for professional learning. In one, three history teachers use their existing expertise about teaching a particular topic to develop it further. In another a whole department shares its ideas about the practice of the history department and the effects of whole school policies but decides that external support could be valuable. In the third case, the head of department is attempting to create a context in which the teacher can deploy her professional skills and the pupils learn history. Our concern is to explore the ways in which history departments can draw on various sources of support to develop their classroom expertise and improve the quality of teaching and learning. The emphasis is firmly on the role of the *department* in these processes of professional development and learning, since the department potentially plays a key role both in professional development that focuses on classroom teaching (Siskin and Little 1995; Helsby 1996) and in enhancing pupil achievement (Ofsted 1997b). We examine two sources of support for professional learning: sources internal to the history department, specifically the existing expertise of the history staff, and sources external to the department, such as findings from Ofsted inspections, research evidence about effective teaching and learning and appraisal. Before examining these two sources of support we consider current approaches to thinking about teacher development.

There is now an extensive and varied literature on professional development and professional learning (Burke 1987; Day and Bell 1991; Fullan and Hargreaves 1992; Calderhead 1993; Eraut 1994). All commentators take as the starting point the ultimate goal of professional development to be enhancing the quality of teaching and thereby the quality of learning by pupils. But once this rather obvious goal is stated, consensus of how to achieve this breaks down – as we found was the case with the simple goal of ITE 'to produce good teachers' (Chapter 2). At issue is the definition of teacher development; what sort of process it is, how it is best achieved, and how teachers and school can engage in it. Hargreaves and Fullan (1992) identify three dominant approaches to understanding teacher development. The first and most common of these sees teacher development as knowledge and skill development. The emphasis here is on giving teachers new strategies for teaching, new knowledge about how children learn and new resources to use in implementing the curriculum. It is the approach that dominates most in-service programmes and courses in this country and 'has become big business' (Hargreaves and Fullan 1992:2).

This approach to teacher development is attractive in its apparent simplicity and appeal to common sense; if pupils are to learn better then teachers need to teach better and the way to achieve this is to provide practical examples of new teaching methods. These methods may be based directly on recent research evidence of what makes for effective teaching but more often are simply attractive in their novelty value. This approach is also attractive as it seems to be clearly focused; it seems to be possible to identify specific problems in classroom practice – differentiation, the needs of the less able, using visual evidence – and target solutions on them. There is no doubt that this approach has a place in in-service training. Suggestions for practice are welcomed by teachers and, especially when they are presented with a means for subsequent follow up and support, can result in improved teaching and learning. However, the returns on this form of teacher development are known to be small in relation to the amount of time, energy and money expended on it (Kerry 1993). Many of the 'new' methods and 'bright ideas' go no further than the seminar room where they were introduced. The reasons why this should be the case lie in the sorts of assumptions that underpin this approach. This represents an essentially deficit view of teachers as people whose existing expertise needs to be replaced by something better – new methods and bright ideas. It assumes that the way professional knowledge is developed is through asking teachers to *apply* ideas developed elsewhere. It assumes that issues of context – the teacher's actual classes and school – are relatively unimportant in making decisions about what sorts of strategies to use. It assumes that teachers need outside experts to tell them what needs development in their practice. It also tends to assume that teacher development and change happens quickly and easily and in immediate response to the presentation of a good idea. For all these reasons this approach to teacher development is flawed and likely to continue to be ineffective (Day 1997).

A second approach views teacher development in terms of reflective self-understanding (Hargreaves and Fullan 1992). The emphasis here is on the connections between the personal and the professional and is grounded in the teacher's own life and actual work. This approach to teacher development assumes that the attitudes and beliefs of teachers are as important as their actions or methods, and that to bring about professional learning means taking account of all these dimensions. One element of this approach, the professional life cycles of teachers, is explored further in Chapter 9, where we discuss the development of individual teachers rather than the role of the department. This approach, unlike the first, assumes a much more positive view of teachers. Its starting point is the teacher, rather than the methods. It assumes that teachers have a major part to play in determining the nature of their own development. It recognizes the importance of context both in personal terms and professional. However, like the first approach, it is abstracted from the realities of classrooms and school cultures. This approach can look more like self-indulgent therapy than professional learning and its outcomes are unpredictable. Because this approach is focused on individuals it is difficult to see how it can stimulate change in a department's practice. None the less, there are emphases in this approach that are attractive and that alert us to some of the complexities of professional development (Day 1997). For example, the emphasis on teachers' attitudes and beliefs is a reminder that their professional development needs are distinctive and will change over time and in different circumstances.

A third approach cited by Hargreaves and Fullan (1992) conceptualizes teacher development as 'ecological change'. This moves the focus away from teachers to the contexts in which they work, and emphasizes the importance of changing the working environments and cultures of schools. Here the central preoccupation is with issues such as school ethos, the ways in which schools are organized, managed and led and the working conditions of teachers. Hargreaves, for example, emphasizes the scope for what he calls a 'culture of collaboration' to 'counter the widespread individualism and isolation that impair and inhibit many teachers' classroom performance and their willingness to change and improve' (Hargreaves 1992:226–7). When they discuss the implications of their research on effective teaching and learning, Cooper and McIntyre identify practical strategies for school and teacher development:

> School development to improve pupils' classroom learning can usefully be thought of in terms of two complementary kinds of strategy. The first of these is concerned with helping teachers to develop their classroom teaching expertise. The other kind of strategy . . . is concerned with minimising the constraints upon teachers' opportunities to foster effective learning in their classrooms.
> (Cooper and McIntyre 1996a:166)

They alert us to the need for conditions conducive to professional learning, and increasingly measures associated with improving schools are identifying the importance of leadership, that ensures 'vigorous action to improve the quality of teaching, pupils' progress and levels of attainment' (Ofsted 1997a:3). However, such whole school approaches are problematic. There are severe difficulties in unpicking the relationships between school effectiveness, school improvement and teacher development (Brown *et al.* 1996) and relatively few examples of the creation of genuinely collaborative cultures in schools.

History departments operate in a context framed by these approaches but we are concerned with what history departments themselves can achieve, although we recognize that they may well be operating within systems and cultures that make their task even more demanding.

In general, history departments and history teachers have under-
estimated the extent to which the department itself can stimulate
professional development. This capacity for generating change in
teaching and learning from the inside is potentially the most
powerful resource any department has. The first example presented
above illustrates how teachers in a department can work together
using their existing expertise in history teaching and learning as the
starting point for development. It shows how, through collaborative planning, teachers can make what they already know and the
skills and abilities they already have explicit both to themselves
and to one another, and use them as the basis for generating improvement (McIntyre and Hagger 1992; Hill 1995). This process,
which assumes that the teachers involved do have something to
contribute and which takes a positive view of those contributions, enables teachers to both learn from each other's extensive professional
knowledge (Brown and McIntyre 1992) and subject that expertise
to critical examination. As Brown and McIntyre observe 'Teachers'
recognition and sharing of their knowledge is thus not only valuable in itself but also potentially a first stage, though a necessary
one for many, towards a self critical process of professional development' (1993:115). Our example demonstrates the potential value of
collaborative planning of a particular unit of work. Other possibilities would be the sharing and discussion, in departmental meetings,
of specific strategies for the teaching of other topics, of ways of
responding to particular learning needs or of appropriate resources
to support certain sorts of goals in history lessons. If the timetable
permitted it, or could be constructed to facilitate it, collaborative
teaching or observation of each other's teaching would be further
opportunities to use what exists as the basis for further development. Despite their potential, these sorts of approaches are not as
common as might be expected. Too often departmental meetings,
for example, are concerned with administration. Heads of department, motivated by a desire to lessen pressures on colleagues and to
lead the department, frequently offer prescriptions for practice. A lack
of time precludes the opportunities for collaborative planning and
teaching and inflexible teaching commitments make observation
impossible. None the less this approach, which explicitly focuses on
the quality of teaching to enhance pupils' learning, is worth fighting
for; it represents a very powerful form of professional learning.

Although this internal source for professional development is a
rich option there are other starting points for development, which
we characterize as *external* to existing expertise. Drawing on such
external sources runs the risks identified earlier associated with the

approach to teacher development as skills and knowledge development. However, we advocate drawing on eternal sources because relying exclusively on existing expertise for *all* development needs and all forms of professional learning runs another, different risk; of being essentially conservative and lacking in challenge. Our argument is that external sources can be used in ways that are consistent with a view of teacher development that starts with existing expertise, but that such sources can be used sensitively to extend that expertise. Here we discuss the possibilities of three such sources: Ofsted inspection findings; research evidence on effective teaching; and research evidence on children's learning in history.

There is no doubt that inspection is seen by statutory bodies as an extremely important force in improving schools and in developing teachers' abilities to promote pupil learning and achievement (Ofsted 1994, 1997a; DfEE 1997c). Some researchers have queried its efficacy (Wilcox and Gray 1996), not least because inspection is required to fulfil a number of purposes, including that of accountability, and these two functions do not sit easily together. Furthermore, the model of schooling embedded in the Ofsted framework for inspection emphasizes management issues, rather than focusing *directly* on teaching and learning and teacher development. Our own scrutiny of reports, like that of Wilcox and Gray, suggests that where teaching and learning is described in findings or as a point for action and development, it is rarely in language that reflects anything of the real nature of these processes. None the less, there are ways in which inspection findings can be of real value to history departments. The recent preoccupation with the development of pupils' writing in history can, in part, be attributed to Ofsted inspection findings. Ofsted's summary of inspection findings in history stated 'that there was insufficient extended writing to support the development of increasingly complex knowledge and understanding' (Ofsted 1995), that 'many pupils still have difficulties in writing in extended prose' and that all pupils 'should be given guidance necessary to enable them to communicate as fully as possible, especially in their written responses' (Ofsted 1996). These findings and the work of the Exeter Extending Literacy Project (Wray and Lewis 1994), have highlighted the demands of Key Element 5 in the National Curriculum, concerned with organizing and communicating historical thinking. The findings have been influential, and there has been a marked response with history departments looking at the types of writing demands they make in their history lessons and the ways in which devices such as writing frames can be used to support analytical and discursive writing – developments that have been supported both by SCAA (1997) and other authors (Counsell 1997).

Another possible external source for professional learning is research evidence on effective teaching. History has not generally been well served in this respect (Pendry and O'Neill 1997) but there has been extensive American research in the field of what is now known as pedagogical content knowledge and some of this has related to history teachers (Gudmundsdottir 1988a,b,c, 1991; Wilson and Wineburg 1988; Wineburg and Wilson 1988a,b; Gudmundsdottir and Shulman 1989; Wilson 1989, 1990a,b; Wineburg 1991a,b). The work of Sigrun Gudmundsdottir, for example, elaborates the models and stories that expert history teachers use to both connect historical ideas and enable them to make selections of ideas and events for their teaching, whereas that of Suzanne Wilson and Sam Wineburg suggests ways that differing conceptions of history as a discipline influenced the teachers; 'the curriculum they were given and the courses they subsequently taught were shaped by what they did and did not know about history' (Wilson and Wineburg 1988:534). This research then suggests that there are a variety of ways in which history teachers draw on their various forms of knowledge, including their understandings of history and their knowledge about learners, to make history interesting and accessible to their pupils. Although this research has been shown to be flawed in its methods and approaches (Marks 1990; Cochran *et al.* 1993; Pendry 1994), it has been very influential and has the potential to promote professional learning in several ways. For example, history departments might use it to support a discussion of the ways in which their view of history affects the sort of history they present to their classes and thus how they choose to interpret the national curriculum (Ball and Bowe 1992). Teachers might discuss the ways in which their different levels of understanding of specific topics affect the ways in which they teach those topics. An individual's expertise in, say, the causes of the French Revolution may well mean that he or she is especially skilful at selecting what is crucial for the pupils and in finding ways of transforming those complex ideas so that they are meaningful to 13-year-olds. History teachers could also usefully draw on research on effective teaching from other subject disciplines. Postlethwaite's work on differentiation in science teaching (Postlethwaite 1993), for example, could provide a stimulus for history teachers to consider the appropriateness in history of the wide range of tactics that he suggests for science teaching. Similarly, Sutton's work on language in science (Sutton 1992) suggests a range of ways in which history teachers can explore the role of language in history teaching.

A final example is provided by one of the research projects sponsored by the Teacher Training Agency (TTA), about raising students' performance in relation to test scores, which makes specific suggestions for teacher actions. Such suggestions, rooted in small scale but thorough research, could provoke discussion amongst history teachers about the appropriateness, feasibility and specific form of these actions in their own classrooms (Hines 1997).

Research about effective learning in history is another possible external resource for history departments. In Chapter 1 we presented some of the findings from Cooper and McIntyre's work on effective teaching and learning in history, and their discussion of pupils' perceptions of the strategies that helped them to learn in history lessons, which could be used as a focus by history departments (Cooper and McIntyre 1996a); so too might research that explicitly explores how children's understanding in history develops. Much of that research has been experimental in nature and not situated in real classrooms, with real teachers and pupils, so it is unlikely to offer immediate solutions to practical pedagogical problems but may stimulate discussion on expectations of pupil attainment in history (Pendry and O'Neill 1997). Some of this research has been mediated to make it accessible and useful to history teachers and departments in reviewing their practice. Publications in the 1980s on empathy (SREB 1986) and sources (Portal 1987), based on the research of Shemilt and others were used extensively by history departments as they developed their understandings of what were then new GCSE assessment requirements, and their strategies for teaching and assessing their pupils. The most extensive current research in history learning is the CHATA project, exploring Concepts of History and Teaching Approaches at Key Stages 2 and 3 (Dickinson *et al.* 1996). The work that has been reported to date has explored in great depth the ways in which children's ideas of explanation in history develop. In some respects this could be described as 'pure' research, into a field about which little has been known to date, and as such it has limited value to practitioners. However, although this may prove to be essentially the case with the first phase of the project, concerned exclusively with pupils' conceptual development, it may be that teachers could none the less use the findings to help them make sense of their own pupils' work or use the research instruments developed by the research team to explore the ways in which their own pupils explain historical events. In addition, the finding that the ideas of some seven-year-olds are as sophisticated as those of many 14-year-olds, might prompt them to examine the demands they make of pupils and whether or not they have sufficiently high expectations of pupils in history, particularly as this mirrors concern reported by Ofsted about teachers' low expectations of some pupils. It could be that the second phase of the CHATA project, linking learning with teaching strategies, may prove to be more directly valuable as a stimulus to professional learning. As with research about effective teaching, research in other subjects has something to offer history teachers. One striking example of this is the extensive work done in science (Driver *et al.* 1985; Claxton 1993) about pupils' existing conceptions of science and the ways in which teachers can effectively understand and use these ideas; some of this work has already influenced work in history. Husbands (1996) has previously argued that the ideas that pupils bring to history lessons have a profound effect on the ways in which they make sense of what they are formally taught, and Pendry's small scale research work (Pendry *et al.* 1997) conducted by PGCE students, has revealed some of the specific ideas that pupils may bring to their learning about, for example, the two world wars or native Americans. Such work could provoke history teachers to discuss what they have observed about the possible effects of such preconceptions, their ways of gaining access to them and the methods that they use to challenge or develop existing understandings.

Suggesting that research based findings – about teaching and learning – might provide the stimulus for professional learning inevitably raises questions about the relationship between research and practice, and the extent to which teaching could become a research-based profession. The claim that it should (Hargreaves 1996a) has been much debated (Gipps 1996; Gray 1996; Hargreaves 1996b; Hammersley 1997), and the TTA has already started funding research projects by practising teachers that it hopes will lead to the development of practice (Teacher Training Agency 1997). Our concern here is more limited. We are suggesting that findings from the research of others (including teacher researchers) might well prove to be valuable sources of insight about teaching and learning in history, with the potential to contribute to professional learning.

We recognize that for history departments to achieve the sorts of professional learning illustrated by our examples will not be easy; so much in the culture and organization of schools work against it and so too do the models of schools and professional development evident in the work of Ofsted and the TTA (Day 1997). None the less, there is significant evidence to suggest that history departments might draw on their own expertise or external stimuli to develop the quality of teaching and learning in history. We are mindful though of the importance of the whole school context on departmental initiatives.

The sort of departmental collegiality implied by the approaches we have discussed is unlikely to even exist, let alone flourish, if the whole school ethos is inimical to it. Both attitudes and policies are likely to be relevant here (Cooper and McIntyre 1996a), and these will reveal themselves in diverse ways: the quality of accommodation available to the history department; the amount of time allocated to the teaching of history; the proportion of the budget allocated to the history department; and decisions about staffing the department. They will be revealed through the leadership and management styles adopted by the senior team, by the overall school ethos and by school approaches to specific initiatives such as appraisal, often vaunted as an opportunity for school and staff development (Brown 1995). It is clear that although appraisal may have very limited success in bringing about teacher development (Wragg *et al.* 1996), it can be of value in professional learning if certain conditions are met. These conditions depend on a view of teachers' expertise similar to that initially developed by Brown and McIntyre (1992). It seems that appraisal is most effective in teacher development when it involves peers and skilled classroom observation that is positive and focused on the teacher's own priorities, and is accorded time and resources. If schools are to have systems of appraisal that genuinely contribute to staff development, then these sorts of characteristics need to be built into the systems they develop.

We have outlined an approach to professional development in history in which a variety of resources, both internal to the department and external to it, are marshalled to ensure a focus on developing the quality of teaching and learning. The evidence suggests that such resources have the capacity to engender professional change; set within the context of a school where such approaches are promoted and celebrated, their power may be substantial. Lawrence Stenhouse described the purpose of education as being something that, 'equips the individual for commitment and action by increasing his understanding. It works most effectively not through authority but through attempting to generate responsibility and caring in a context of emancipation' (Stenhouse 1978:741). The same holds true for teacher education.

9

DEVELOPING HISTORY TEACHERS AND HISTORY TEACHING: CASE STUDIES IN PROFESSIONAL LEARNING

In the previous chapter we argued that the history department has a key role to play in developing the quality of history teaching and learning, and that there are both internal and external sources of support for departments in this complex and difficult task. In this chapter we move the focus from history departments to the *teachers* who make them up. Our reason for doing this is two-fold. In the first place we are concerned with the relationship between the sorts of professional development we have already sketched, which focus on classrooms and on learning, and teachers' career development. There is confusion between the two in much of the research and general literature: professional development is seen as the route to career advancement, to higher salaries, and, in the classic formulation, 'beyond' the subject. Clearly, career development brings with it the need to acquire new and additional skills in discharging whole-school and management responsibilities. The skills involved in managing a department are different from those involved in teaching pupils effectively, demanding high level skills of designing curricula, managing personnel and, increasingly, an awareness of whole-school and national policy developments. The skills required for headship and deputy headship are different again, involving the ability to think in strategic terms about the development of the school as an institution and to mediate the relationships between the school and its environment. Characteristically, however, in schools those who discharge middle and senior management responsibilities *are also classroom teachers*, and they retain responsibilities to pupils to teach

Table 9.1 Huberman's schematic model of the teacher career cycle

Years of teaching	Themes/phases
1–3	Career entry: 'survival'/'discovery'
	↓
4–6	Stabilization
	↓
	Focusing
7–18	Experimentation/activism Reassessment/self-doubts
	↓ ↓
19–30	Serenity/relational distance Conservatism
31–40	↘ Disengagement: ↙
	'serene' or 'bitter'

their subject effectively and imaginatively. This can produce tensions, well documented in research literature, between their teaching and managerial responsibilities. The relationship between career and professional development is neither straightforward nor simple.

Our second concern is to set teachers' professional development as *history* teachers in the context of their professional life cycles (Burn 1995). There is now considerable literature exploring the relationship between teachers' jobs and their lives. Sikes (1985) and Huberman (1992), following Levinson *et al.* (1979), sketch what seem to be five phases in the teacher's life cycle, each distinguished by the different objectives teachers have in their work, the priority they accord it in relation to their lives and the kinds of relationships they construct with students and colleagues. Huberman's work on Swiss teachers identified five phases of a teacher career cycle (Table 9.1). The first phase, lasting for perhaps one to three years is characterized as being concerned with 'survival' and 'discovery', as new teachers establish themselves in the classroom: 'a sense of being overwhelmed, continual trial and error, vacillation between excessive strictness and permissiveness, exhaustion' (Huberman 1992:129; Hannam 1981). The second phase, 'stabilization' is characterized by 'commitment to the profession, consolidation of a basic pedagogical repertoire . . . and . . . experimentation outside the classroom in order to get a better shot at the instructional outcomes one is after' (Huberman 1992:129). The third phase is generally characterized as 'focusing': for some individuals this will be a matter of identifying and working towards specific career goals – promotion, for example

– whereas for others it will involve a 'reassessment' of career in the context of life, so that teachers might focus on their out-of-school lives and commitments (Sikes 1985:52; Huberman 1992:130). Some teachers are firmly established on the path to promotion to senior management, whereas others, perhaps genuinely or perhaps as an excuse for their failure to achieve promotion, now profess a wish to 'stay in the classroom' (Sikes 1985:52; Huberman 1992:130). There are important gender differences at this phase. Many women in their thirties may have chosen to make their career as a teacher second-ary to their career as a parent (Sikes 1997). This third phase gives way to a fourth. Those who have become 'focused activists' achieve, or reconcile themselves to, their career goals, whereas those who have reassessed their teaching commitments in relation to other goals settle into conservatism. The final phase, characterized by progressive 'disengagement' will tend to be either 'serene' or 'embittered'. Teachers in these last two stages are likely to be relatively conservative, dis-inclined to pedagogic innovation (Fullan and Hargreaves 1994:38). It follows that teachers' professional learning needs in relation to their development as classroom practitioners will vary throughout their career life cycles (Day 1993a; Burn 1995). We examine the relationships between teacher development and professional devel-opment, between professional development and teaching quality, through a case study of the history department at Edgefield High School. Although Edgefield is a fictional example, it draws extensively on a series of case studies of staff attitudes and perceptions of pro-fessional development in comprehensive schools after the National Curriculum (Becker 1970; Huberman 1989, 1992; Ball and Bowe 1992; Burn 1995).

Edgefield High School

Edgefield High School is a mixed comprehensive of 1150 pupils aged 11–18, including 170 in the sixth form. The school, on the edge of a large town, draws its pupils from a variety of housing types and social groups. It was built in the 1960s as a secondary modern school, becoming a comprehensive in 1973. There have been a series of building programmes in the 1970s and 1980s and the buildings are an unprepossessing mixture of styles, and there are mobile classrooms on the playing field. Their presence is an indication of the school's recent history; it is popular and has become more so over the past few years. The school has increased in size by almost a fifth in five years as parents have increasingly chosen to send their children here at age 11, and as the post-16 staying on rate has improved. The intake, which was six forms of entry five years ago, grew to seven forms of entry and, in the current Year 7 comprises eight forms.

The Edgefield history department

The history department is regarded as successful and lively. All pupils study National Curriculum history for two of the timetabled 25 periods in Years 7, 8 and 9 and there are history field trips in the summer term each year. The subject is optional in Years 10 and 11 but always attracts enough GCSE pupils for the school to run two groups in each year, each group allocated three periods a week. There are always enough A-level students to run one large group and, as in the current Year 12, sometimes to run two groups. Examination results both at GCSE and A level are typically above both the LEA and school averages. The school was inspected by Ofsted during the past academic year and the history report was generally good; teaching was found to be always satisfactory and sometimes good, and pupil attainment was noted as being above the national average. The report particularly praised the leadership of the head of department and commended the department for its imaginative cooperation with the special needs coordinator in making provision for pupils with learning difficulties. However, the report felt that the department's accommodation was less than ideal. Despite the existence of a history department office with carefully filed resources and well ordered shelves of reference and inspection copies of textbooks, teaching accommodation was scattered and there were only two specialist history rooms, other teachers being required to teach in mobile classrooms of rooms theoretically dedicated to other subjects. Weaknesses were highlighted in assessment and particularly in recording and reporting, which were described as 'haphazard'. The Ofsted report also noted that the department was making inadequate use of information technology to support work in history. In informal feedback to the headteacher and chair of governors, the Ofsted team raised further issues. They felt that pupils in some classes were not being adequately challenged and implied that these were taught by a long-serving member of the department, and they felt that there were weaknesses in some of the A-level teaching.

Five teachers teach history at Edgefield. Beth is the head of department. Now 32, she has been teaching for nine years and has been head of history at Edgefield for five years. Beth enjoys her teaching and finds running her department stimulating, although like many heads of department she finds the burden of teaching 22 periods alongside her administrative and management responsibilities challenging. There are two other full-time history teachers. Andy, now 26, has been teaching for three years – Edgefield is his first post. He is an enthusiastic and lively teacher who is clear that he would like to move on to run his own department. He has become active in history teaching outside his own classroom; he was a mentor for the student teachers on placement at Edgefield last year and also undertook some GCSE examining at the end of last year. Beth and Andy generally get on well. They share an enthusiasm for the subject and for teaching it well, which means that they can have lively conversations about strategies and classroom issues. Eddie is the other full-time history teacher. Now in his fifties he has taught at Edgefield since he began teaching thirty years ago. He was born and grew up locally, and like all teachers who teach for a long time in the same school he feels that he knows the area and the pupils 'inside out'; some of the pupils he now teaches are the children of those he taught in the past. Eddie is the school's examinations secretary, an administrative task he discharges with blustery, if somewhat overbearing, efficiency. He has been chair of the Staff Common Room Association and a teacher governor for many years. Eddie teaches 22 periods a week, mostly in Years 7–9. His history lessons are popular with pupils and he is noted for his ability to work with the less able; he tells historical stories with animation and warmth. Eddie has the air of someone who has 'seen it all'; he is cynical about innovation, and in consequence tends to pay lip service to recent innovations such as the assessment and curriculum demands of the National Curriculum in history. Beth assumes that it was Eddie's teaching at Key Stage 3 that was felt by Ofsted to lack challenge. She feels that Eddie should be prepared to rethink his approaches to teaching history, but he has a variety of local outside interests into which he invests considerable time and energy.

Two other members of staff contribute to history teaching. Colin is deputy head responsible for the curriculum at Edgefield. He has been teaching for 16 years, and was himself a head of history before becoming a deputy and before the introduction of the National Curriculum. As Beth, Andy and Colin share the A-level teaching, Beth is reasonably sure that it was Colin's A-level teaching that was cited as relatively weak by Ofsted. Colin is clear that his main role is in the management of the school. He teaches eight periods a week, but his management responsibilities, and over the last eight months or so his interviews for headships in other schools, means that he misses many lessons, which have to be 'covered'. When he is present, he tends to rely on work done by others: using worksheets and activities planned, especially, by Andy. His tendency to deploy what she sees as 'management speak', and his increasing reliance on Andy have begun to irritate Beth. She feels that he is out of touch with recent developments in history teaching. The last member of the department is Diane, a 45-year-old part-time teacher who has three young children. Diane moved to Edgefield two years ago when her husband's career brought him to the area. She is a very experienced teacher, and although she enjoys history teaching she was trained as an English specialist. Diane's timetable is normally constructed to fill gaps: so her load this year, as last, includes English and geography as well as the six periods of history she teaches. Diane rarely attends history team meetings: if she *is* able to attend departmental meetings, she feels that her identity lies more with the English team.

Professional development in the Edgefield history department

The Edgefield history department is not unusual; it may, if anything be rather more coherent than many history departments. Some of the features of the Edgefield department echo the findings of school and departmental effectiveness studies; there is strong leadership from an active head of department and there is an efficient system of resource management (Myers 1996:8–11). But as a focus of professional development, it is clear that the needs of the members of the department differ sharply because of their different concerns and aspirations and because of their different career trajectories and experiences.

Andy is clear about his next career step: he would like to become a head of history. His success in this is likely to depend partly on his continued success as a classroom teacher at Edgefield, but also the opportunities that Beth is able to offer Andy to become more closely involved in the development of history within the school. Andy's involvement in mentoring, his work as a GCSE examiner and his collaboration with Beth in planning lower school history fieldwork are all experiences that will help to focus Andy's development in the areas that are required for his career: on the pedagogy of the subject and on the management of the subject within the context of the school. This concern with the classroom and curriculum makes the professional development agenda for Andy relatively clear-cut.

Beth can help to involve him more in the running of the department. The school could support Andy by ensuring his continued
involvement in mentoring, and might facilitate his contact with
outside agencies. He will develop a network through his mentoring,
but should be encouraged to attend history in-service education
and training (INSET) provided by the LEA and might be encouraged
to undertake advanced study part-time at the local university. At
some point, Andy will need to register for the National Professional
Qualification for Subject Leaders (NPQSL) (Teacher Training Agency
1997). There are specific tasks that Andy could be assigned to undertake in order to prepare him for these developments, that address
the department's needs. Beth, in particular, might ask Andy to lead
the development worked highlighted by Ofsted's criticism of the
department's approach to IT, perhaps enlisting the advice of the
LEA history inspector on departments in other schools where Andy
could visit to observe good practice. Tension in Andy's professional
development is only likely to arise if the head, also concerned to
ensure that Andy's career develops, asks him to undertake a substantial task *outside* the department; as an assistant head of year,
perhaps, or as assistant to the head of careers guidance. However,
Andy's own personal aspirations to develop his career in the first
instance inside the discipline is likely to have been addressed through
appraisal, whether formal or informal (Wragg *et al.* 1996).

The relationship between career and professional development is
less close for the other members of the department. Beth is a successful head of history but is unsure of her career aspirations. Other
commentators have noted that teachers in their thirties face particular dilemmas in sorting conflicting priorities (Sikes 1985; Spencer 1995). Beth is committed to her subject. One possibility would
be for her to seek to develop her career through history. She believes that she would enjoy LEA advisory work and that she would
be good at it, but she also enjoys the day-to-day contact with pupils
and her friendship with her current LEA adviser has suggested to
her that she might find the business unit ethos which underpins the
LEA's work unattractive. Beth's headteacher thinks that Beth should
contemplate a move into senior management. She is very keen that
women should aspire to senior roles in the schools and feels that
Beth has excellent management skills, which need further development through additional experiences and training. The head sees
Beth's move into senior management as unproblematic: it was what
she did and seems to her to be a natural career progression. Beth is,
though, discouraged by Colin's example as a deputy head; she feels
that this role distances him from the subject. Finally, Beth considers

her career in the context of her life. She has been in a long-term relationship, and her partner would like them to marry as a prelude to beginning a family. Further promotion might be 'detrimental to other aspects of [her] . . . life' (Sikes 1985:48). Beth is ambivalent about this. She enjoys her work and has always laid great importance on her own professional success, but her older sisters, both now married with children, are personal reminders to her that she might, as she moves into her mid-thirties, want to reorient her personal and professional lives. So, for Beth there are tensions between what she sees as her professional development and her career development. It is clear that she will have to make choices, but it is much less clear how the school, or the department, can support her in making these choices. What is important is that Beth is helped to see the choices she must make, and that her choice is reflected in the staff development provision that is made. However, since those to whom she might most readily turn for career guidance do not see her choices as being difficult, she is unlikely to find it easy to acquire supportive career counselling.

Colin, like Andy, has a clear career goal; he wants to be a head-teacher. He came into teaching because he wanted to teach and enjoyed his subject, but these initial motivations have been subsumed by his career development. Colin represents one of Beth's possible career choices; but Beth sees Colin as effectively dependent on others in his history teaching. She believes that Colin sees school as a management tool for the delivery of certain goals (Wilcox and Gray 1996) rather than as a collection of classrooms in which teachers and pupils work. Beth is particularly irritated by Colin's reaction to her discussion of the Ofsted criticism of his A-level teaching. He said that he was 'hurt' by the comments but realized that he simply couldn't do everything and was pleased that the report had praised the consultative style of the senior management team. There is a sharp tension between what Colin sees as his professional learning needs, which are grounded in management and strategic thinking, and what his head of department sees as his need to focus on classroom teaching. She feels that she must interest him again in classroom teaching, and, as she puts it that she must 're-educate' him about the subject and its demands. Beth might persuade Colin that she, or Andy, should observe his lessons and he some of theirs in return. Discussion of these observations could focus on classroom approaches and the relationships between the teachers' strategies and pupils' historical development. These discussions should be expected to be fairly technical and sophisticated; they would be based on the assumption that what was being exchanged were professional insights

drawing on experience and, where appropriate, the relationship between what is happening in Edgefield history classrooms and recent
research findings.

For Diane and Eddie, careers are parts of their wider lives. Diane
is a teacher, mother and wife. She is, as a professional, keen to do a
'good job with the pupils', but as she puts it, her attitude to her pupils
has shifted now that she is a mother: she puts the demands of her
own children first (Sikes 1997). Teaching is more than a source of
'pin-money' but she juggles her work and domestic commitments and
so she works part-time. She teaches history, geography and English.
She is aware that she is relying on her professional experience as
the sole resource for her thinking but that this is not sufficiently
challenging to her. As a part-timer, she does not attend all INSET
sessions or departmental meetings; and she is in any case unsure
which department's meetings she should attend. If she reads professional journals, it will be those that relate to her English teaching.
She feels that she does not really 'know' enough history and that
her grasp of the intricacies of National Curriculum history is tenuous.
Yet Diane teaches history, and for her pupils it does not matter that
she is a part-timer teaching one of her subsidiary subjects. Diane is
an enthusiast for teaching the pupils she is assigned, but the task of
supporting her is complex; she is, in many respects, a 'marginal'
history teacher. If the school, or Beth, is to support her effectively,
then strategies need to be designed that take account of Diane's
view of the place of teaching in her life and her need to be able to
relate to material in three curriculum areas. She needs succinct and
focused guidance, which allows her to develop history teaching
strategies that reflect her very considerable classroom expertise but
uncertainty about history.

Eddie is a history specialist. Like Diane he has a broad range of
interests outside teaching; 'teaching' is one of the things he does. He
thinks of his work far more in terms of the pupils he teaches than
the subjects he is teaching them. His view of pedagogy is uncompli-
cated, being based on strategies and approaches he developed 30 years
ago, so that his lip-service to the formal demands of the National
Curriculum and assessment is a form of passive resistance. Eddie is
not disenchanted from Beth's department, nor oppositional, but he
poses some challenges in terms of professional development. He
may become oppositional if Beth uses the Ofsted comments on his
teaching as too direct a criticism of his approach to standards and
expectations. It is impossible to connect professional development
for Eddie or Diane to notions of career development since neither
wishes to advance a career. Equally, 'deficit model' in-service training

is more likely than not to provoke such teachers further into 'withdrawal' or 'oppositionism' since it would not build on their obvious strengths. Instead, professional development needs to be founded on respect for their professional craft knowledge while acknowledging their needs. Evidence suggests (Hargreaves 1992; Burn 1995) that teachers in Eddie's and Diane's position are likely to benefit where time is devoted to collaborative and *focused* departmental discussion; for example, through group evaluation of available textbooks, or carefully structured collaborative planning and creation of resources. Beth's skills in departmental leadership would be essential in such activities so that the focus on enhancing classroom learning is retained, but such activities would be firmly rooted in Diane's and Eddie's experiences of their own classrooms and what 'works' in them.

Conclusion

The Edgefield history department exemplifies the complexity of planning for professional development. There is a great deal of evidence to suggest that effective teacher development depends on the generation of participative and collaborative cultures of schooling (Hargreaves 1992; Fullan and Hargreaves 1994). Generalizing from such researchers, commentators have sought to urge the establishment of models of continuing learning, which allow teachers to become the designers of their own self-directed professional development (Clark 1992; Somekh *et al.* 1994). The experiences we have discussed suggest that this is only partially true. It is indeed the case that teachers' experiences and career trajectories generate fundamentally different demands for professional learning and that much effective change can only be generated by classroom practitioners. But several of our teachers demonstrate, as does empirical research (Day 1993b; Burn 1995) that delegating responsibility exclusively to individuals or groups for their own development is unlikely to be effective. In an educational context characterized by a centralized curriculum, centrally managed national qualifications, regular school inspection and external scrutiny through the publication of examination results, rather more is needed. Heads of department must ensure that time is made available in departmental meetings for *focused* discussion of classroom teaching; the central activity of the department. Senior managers and experienced teachers, like departments, must accept their responsibilities to renew and examine their own classroom practice. Teachers should accept that observation and review of their teaching is not simply to be left to their initial training or the burden of appraisal and inspection. The relationship between subject knowledge, pedagogy and understandings of children's learning must be an overt focus for discussion in departments. Classroom-focused professional development is not a right for teachers; it is a responsibility they owe their pupils. Our contention is that enhancing the quality of teaching in history depends crucially on continued professional learning that is classroom focused, acknowledges the realities of accountability against which all teachers operate and is grounded in dialogue about effective pedagogy and outcomes in the subjects of the curriculum.

10

CONCLUSION: HISTORY TEACHING, CLASSROOM LEARNING AND PROFESSIONAL DEVELOPMENT

We began this book by describing three history lessons, each distinctive in content, style and outcomes, which together demonstrated the complexity of teaching and learning history in schools. Throughout the book we have explored the ways in which ITE, the induction process for NQTs and further professional development could contribute to enhancing the quality of teaching and thus of pupil learning. At each stage we have discussed the ways in which the processes of learning to teach are distinctive and complex. We have outlined principles and explored practices, grounded in the lived realities of history classrooms and in the outcomes of research, that we believe could contribute to the development of history teaching.

We write this book at a time when the position of history in schools is under threat, as it has been at other times in the past (Price 1968; Booth 1969; Sylvester 1994). This time the threat is derived from increasingly vocational and instrumental emphases in the curriculum as economic and political pressures on education are sharply increasing. At the same time, history remains a deeply contested school subject. History teachers approach the subject from a variety of perspectives, derived themselves from different models of teaching and learning in the discipline. Both the history of the discipline and its epistemology have been thoroughly discussed and debated over the past 30 years (Hexter 1972; Ferro 1984; Jenkins 1991, 1996; Lee 1991; Schama 1992; Sylvester 1994). We are not concerned here with contributing to either of those literatures but we are concerned with exploring the relationship between the nature of the subject and professional development of history teachers. Articulating a rationale for history in the school curriculum and debating that which is contestable about the subject are activities that both promote professional learning and development and are also a necessary component of them.

Debate about the subject has been dominated by two approaches to history. The most influential tradition in history teaching has been what David Sylvester has called the Great Tradition; 'this tradition of history teaching was clear cut in both its aims and its methodology. The history teacher's role was didactically active . . . the body of knowledge . . . was mainly political history with some social and economic aspects, and it was mainly British history with some European history from Julius Caesar to 1914' (Sylvester 1994:9). Slater has described the characteristics of the Great Tradition in these terms: 'content was largely British, or rather Southern English; Celts looked in to starve, emigrate or rebel; the North to invent looms or work in mills; abroad was of interest once it was part of the empire; foreigners were either, sensibly, allies, or, rightly, defeated' (Slater 1989:1). More recently, and particularly after 1970, this Great Tradition was challenged, principally through the work of the Schools Council History 13–16 Project (SCHP 1976). This influential curriculum development project expressed a philosophy for the teaching of history in schools that was to be 'as similar as possible to history as philosophers conceived it and as the best professionals practised it' (Sylvester 1994:16). It was characterized by a concern for the historian's methods and the conceptual structure of the discipline rather than for history as a body of knowledge (Pendry 1981). In the classroom, SCHP approaches were reflected in an emphasis on the development of historical skills, in the analysis and evaluation of historical sources and in the explicit focus on historical concepts such as causation, change and empathy. GCSE and the National Curriculum for history drew on both of these traditions, although each, ultimately, represented a somewhat uneasy compromise between them.

Neither tradition is wholly unproblematic. No one would deny that the acquisition of knowledge about the past is an important reason for studying history. Teachers want pupils to build up such knowledge; but this is far from straightforward. There *is* simply too much history for any child to learn, and some selection has to be made. Once that is acknowledged, there have to be clear, publicly agreed criteria for selecting the history that is to be taught. Some criteria emphasize the importance of history in transmitting an understanding of national traditions and culture, and others its 'compensatory, oppositional function' (Slater 1995:130; Visram 1994). These different positions represent different perspectives on the nature of culture and historical knowledge. Consider two examples. How is a history teacher to teach about slavery? Is he or she to present the stories of slavers or of slaves, and with what emphasis? Now what of child labour in early Victorian factories? There are different versions of these experiences, they are all, in different ways part of our culture, but the significance they have, and the ways we look at them are different; they are *contested*. Was child labour in early Victorian Britain an economic necessity or a great cruelty? Historians, politicians and the rest of us disagree about these things. We cannot duck that disagreement. Learning about the disagreement, exploring the reasons for it, is part of learning about our 'culture'. The disagreements have to be explored as much as the achievements have to be celebrated or the iniquities condemned. There simply is no unchanging version of our past, fixed and agreed for all time, and to assert that such a version exists is blatantly incorrect.

The competing tradition, with its emphasis on historical skills and concepts is no more clear-cut. Clearly, pupils need to acquire skills in order to develop their historical understanding, and, in particular, need to develop a grasp of the concept of evidence in order to construct arguments, defend the defensible and attack the indefensible. However, if school history is seen as *largely* concerned with primary evidence, so that pupils come to historical sources without a sense of the way in which others have approached them, the outcomes are likely to be disappointing. It may even be the case that pupils fail to develop any understanding of what historical sources are. As Shemilt notes, 'In practice, many adolescents required to use primary sources are given the means to answer questions they have not yet learned to ask' (Shemilt 1987:43). 'The length, the conceptual and linguistic difficulties of many sources, and in some cases their sheer boredom, make it impossible for pupils to make any realistic appraisal of their significance' (Husbands 1996:17). In many cases, the 'skills' themselves operate at a lamentably low level. A preoccupation with primary historical evidence underplays the importance of narrative structures, which provide the framework within which questions are posed and answers developed. No historian would embark on a historical investigation without considering what others had written. Finally, the focus on developing the 'skills of the historian' neglects the extent to which history is a form of public knowledge; the development of 'evidential skills' in effect distracts attention from historical content.

Our understanding of teaching and learning history is simply put. We question the extent to which there is a single, easily understood and easily transmitted culture. Our language and culture have been shaped and enriched by a series of invasions and migrations. We want children to understand this history and this culture, and we believe that in a modern society understanding the diversity of our society is an important part of understanding society itself. Equally, to achieve these understandings, requires the development of skills in understanding, analysing, questioning and challenging what others have written.

These goals create tensions. John Slater, to whose own thinking we owe an enormous debt, drawing on the work of Peter Lee and others, points up the distinction between 'extrinsic' goals of history teaching (the notion of history being deployed in the wider service of some social goal) and its 'intrinsic' aims (related to the notion that the study of the past is legitimate in its own terms) (Lee 1991; Slater 1995:124–6). Some of the extrinsic claims made for school history, and some of the goals that are set for it, are particularly grand, but it is important to remember, as Lee notes, that, 'the reason for teaching history is not that it changes society but that it changes pupils' (Lee 1991). There is an inevitable tension between the expectation that history will play a part in the transmission of a common culture and the notion that it will provide a mechanism for subjecting received ideas to critical scrutiny. John Slater identifies the tension between those who regard history as being *predominantly* about extrinsic, 'socializing' goals and those who believe its function as being concerned with predominantly intrinsic, 'mind-opening' goals; declaring his own preference for the latter (Slater 1989:16).

In some respects these issues seem to take us a long way from classrooms but in other respects they are absolutely essential to the ways teachers work in the classroom. The ideas we have of the nature of history, its purpose and content condition the way we interact with pupils and assess the outcomes of their work and are thus an important element in professional development and learning. History more than any other subject is about values. The examination and articulation of these values in relation to and on the basis of classroom experience is itself an essential dimension of professional learning in history.

BIBLIOGRAPHY

Abbott, I., Evans, L., Goodyear, R. and Pritchard, A. (1995) *Hammer and Tongue: The Training of Technology Teachers*. Warwick: University of Warwick Teacher Development Research and Dissemination Unit.

Alexander, R. (1984) Innovation and continuity in the initial teacher education curriculum, in R. Alexander, M. Craft and E. Lynch (eds) *Change in Teacher Education: Context and Provision since Robbins*. London: Holt, Rinehart and Winston.

Allsop, T. and Benson, A. (1997) *Mentoring for Science Teachers*. Buckingham: Open University Press.

Ashby, R. and Lee, P. J. (1987) Children's concepts of empathy and understanding in history, in C. Portal (ed.) *The History Curriculum for Teachers*. Lewes: Falmer.

Ball, S. J. and Bowe, R. (1992) Subject departments and the 'implementation' of National Curriculum policy: an overview of the issues. *Journal of Curriculum Studies*, 24(2): 97–115.

Barker, B. (1978) Understanding in the classroom, in A. K. Dickinson and P. J. Lee (eds) *History Teaching and Historical Understanding*. London: Heinemann.

Barnes, D. (1976) *From Communication to Curriculum*. Harmondsworth: Penguin.

Barrett, L., Barton, L., Furlong, J., Galvin, C., Miles, S. and Whitty, G. (1993) *Initial Teacher Education in England and Wales: A Typography*, the Modes of Teacher Education Project. London: Goldsmith College, University of London.

Barton, R. and Elliott, J. (1996) Designing a competency based framework for assessing student teachers: the UEA approach, in D. Hustler and D. McIntyre (eds) *Developing Competent Teachers*. London: David Fulton.

Becker, H. (1970) The career of the Chicago schoolmaster, in H. Becker (ed.) *Sociological Work: Method and Substance*. Chicago: Aldine.

Benton, P. (ed.) (1990) *The Oxford Internship Scheme: Integration and Partnership in Initial Teacher Education*. London: Calouste Gulbenkian Foundation.

Berrill, M. (1992) Structured mentoring and the development of teaching skill, in M. Wilkin (ed.) *Mentoring in Schools*. London: Kogan Page.

Bird, T., Anderson, L. M., Sullivan, B. A. and Swidler, S. A. (1993) Pedagogical balancing acts: attempts to influence prospective teachers' beliefs. *Teaching and Teacher Education*, 9(3): 253–67.

Booth, M. (1987) Ages and concepts: a critique of the Piagetian approach to History teaching, in C. Portal (ed.) *The History Curriculum for Teachers*. Lewes: Falmer.

Booth, M. B. (1969) *History Betrayed?* Harlow: Longman.

Booth, M. B. (1993) *The Teaching and Learning of History: A British Perspective*. Göteborgs Universitet: Projektet Europa och Läroboken.

Brooks, V. and Sikes, P. with Husbands, C. (1997) *The Good Mentor Guide: Initial Teacher Education in Secondary Schools*. Buckingham: Open University Press.

Brown, R. (1995) *Managing the Learning of History*. London: David Fulton.

Brown, S. and McIntyre, D. (1992) *Making Sense of Teaching*. Buckingham: Open University Press.

Brown, S., Riddell, S. and Duffield, J. (1996) Responding to pressures: a study of four secondary schools, in P. Woods (ed.) *Contemporary Issues in Teaching and Learning*. London: Routledge.

Bruner, J. (1986) *Actual Minds: Possible Worlds*. Harvard: Harvard University Press.

Bruner, J. (1987) The transactional self, in J. Bruner and H. Haste (eds) *Making Sense: The Child's Construction of the World*. London: Methuen.

Bullough, R. V. Jr (1992) Beginner teacher curriculum decision making, personal teaching metaphors and teacher education. *Teaching and Teacher Education*, 8(3): 239–52.

Bullough, R. V. Jr with Stokes, D. K. (1994) Analysing teaching metaphors in preservice teacher education as a means for encouraging professional development. *American Educational Research Journal*, 31(1): 197–224.

Burke, P. (1987) *Teacher Development: Induction, Renewal and Redirection*. Lewes: Falmer.

Burn, K. (1992) Collaborative teaching, in M. Wilkin (ed.) *Mentoring in Schools*. London: Kogan Page.

Burn, K. (1995) *Teachers' Perceptions and Experience of Professional Development: A Case-study of a School Department During an Academic Year*. MSc in Educational Studies dissertation, Department of Educational Studies, University of Oxford.

Burn, K. (1997) Collaborative teaching, in D. McIntyre (ed.) *Teacher Education Research in a New Context*. London: Paul Chapman.

Bush, T., Coleman, M., Wall, D. and West-Burnham, J. (1996) Mentoring and continuing professional development, in D. McIntyre and H. Hagger (eds) *Mentors in Schools: Developing the Profession of Teaching*. London: David Fulton.

Calderhead, J. (1984) *Teachers' Classroom Decision Making*. London: Holt, Rinehart and Winston.

Calderhead, J. (ed.) (1987) *Exploring Teachers' Thinking*. London: Cassell.

Calderhead, J. (1988) The development of knowledge structures in learning to teach, in J. Calderhead (ed.) *Teachers' Professional Learning*. London: Falmer.

Calderhead, J. (1989) Reflective teaching and teacher education. *Teaching and Teacher Education*, 15(1): 43–51.

Calderhead, J. (1992) Induction: a research perspective on the professional growth of the newly qualified teacher, in J. Calderhead and J. Lambert (eds) *The Induction of Newly Appointed Teachers*. London: General Teaching Council Initiative for England and Wales.

Calderhead, J. (1993) The contribution of research on teachers' thinking to the professional development of teachers, in C. Day, J. Calderhead and P. Denicolo (eds) *Research on Teacher Thinking: Understanding Professional Development*. London: Falmer.

Calderhead, J. and Robson, M. (1991) Images of teaching: student teachers' early conceptions of classroom practice. *Teaching and Teacher Education*, 17(1): 1–8.

Calderhead, J. and Shorrock, S. B. (1997) *Understanding Teacher Education*. London: Falmer.

Cameron-Jones, M. and O'Hara, P. (1997) Support and challenge in teacher education. *British Educational Research Journal*, 23(1): 15–23.

Carney, S. and Hagger, H. (1996) Working with beginning teachers: the impact on schools, in D. McIntyre and H. Hagger (eds) *Mentors in Schools: Developing the Profession of Teaching*. London: David Fulton.

Chancellor, V. (1970) *History for their Masters: History in the School Textbook 1800–1914*. London: Penguin.

Clark, C. (1992) Teachers as designers in self-directed professional development, in A. Hargreaves and M. Fullan (eds) *Understanding Teacher Development*. London: Cassell.

Clark, C. M. and Yinger, R. J. (1979) Three studies of teacher planning, paper presented at the annual meeting of the American Educational Research Association, San Francisco.

Claxton, G. (1993) Minitheories: a preliminary model for learning science, in P. J. Black and A. M. Lucas (eds) *Children's Informal Ideas in Science*. London: Routledge.

Cochran, K. F., DeRuiter, J. A. and King, R. A. (1993) Pedagogical content knowing: an integrative model for teacher preparation. *Journal of Teacher Education*, 44(4): 263–72.

Coltham, J. B. and Fines, J. (1970) *Educational Objectives for the Study of History*. London: Historical Association.

Comyns, R. (1996) Voice demands on student teachers. *Voice Care*, 4(2): 5–9.

Constable, H. and Norton, J. (1994) Student teachers and their professional encounters, in I. Reid, H. Constable and R. Griffiths (eds) *Teacher Education Reform: Current Research*. London: Paul Chapman.

Cooper, P. and McIntyre, D. (1995) The crafts of the classroom: teachers' and students' accounts of the knowledge underpinning effective teaching and learning in classrooms. *Research Papers in Education*, 10(2): 181–216.

Cooper, P. and McIntyre, D. (1996a) *Effective Teaching and Learning: Students' and Teachers' Perspectives*. Buckingham: Open University Press.

Cooper, P. and McIntyre, D. (1996b) The importance of power-sharing in classroom learning, in M. Hughes (ed.) *Teaching and Learning in Changing Times*. Oxford: Blackwell.

Counsell, C. (1997) *Analytical and Discursive Writing in History at Key Stage 3: A Practical Guide*. London: Historical Association.

Crosson, M. and Shiu, C. (1995) Evaluation and judgement, in B. Jaworski and A. Watson (eds) *Mentoring in Mathematics Teaching*. London: Falmer.

Davies, C. (1996) *What is English Teaching?* Buckingham: Open University Press.

Davison, J. (1997) The transition from student teacher to NQT, in S. Capel, M. Leask and T. Turner (eds) *Starting to Teach in the Secondary School*. London: Routledge.

Day, C. (1993a) The importance of learning biography in supporting teacher development: an empirical study, in C. Day, J. Calderhead and P. Denicolo (eds) *Research on Teacher Thinking: Understanding Professional Development*. Lewes: Falmer.

Day, C. (1993b) Reflection: a necessary but not a sufficient condition for teacher development. *British Education Research Journal*, 19(i): 43–83.

Day, C. (1997) Being a professional in schools and universities: limits, purposes and possibilities for development. *British Educational Research Journal*, 23(2): 193–208.

Day, C. and Bell, L. (1991) *Managing the Professional Development of Teachers*. Buckingham: Open University Press.

DES (1972) *Teacher Education and Training* (The James Report). London: HMSO.

DES (1984) *Initial Teacher Training: Approval of Courses (Circular 3/84)*. London: HMSO.

DES (1990) *National Curriculum History Working Group Final Report*. London: HMSO.

DfE (1992) *Initial Teacher Training (Secondary Phase) Circular No 9/92, Circular No 35/92 (Welsh Office)*. London: HMSO.

DfE (1993) *Initial Teacher Education: Primary, Approval of Courses (Circular 14/93)*. London: HMSO.

DfEE (1994) The National Curriculum: History Statutory Orders. London: HMSO.

DfEE (1997a) *Standards for the Award of Qualified Teacher Status (Circular 1/97)*. London: DfEE.

DfEE (1997b) *Separate Tables: Statistics on Women and Men in Education, Training and Employment*. London: HMSO.

DfEE (1997c) *Excellence in Schools*. London: HMSO.

Dickinson, A. K., Ashby, R. and Lee, P. J. (1996) 'There were no facts in those days': children's ideas about historical explanation, in M. Hughes (ed.) *Teaching and Learning in Changing Times*. Oxford: Blackwell.

Draper, J. *et al.* (1992) *A Study of Probationary Teachers*. Edinburgh: Scottish Office Education Department.

Driver, R., Guesne, E. and Tiberghien, A. (1985) *Children's Ideas in Science*. Milton Keynes: Open University Press.

Dunkin, M. (1996) Types of errors in synthesising research in education. *Review of Educational Research*, 66(2): 87–97.

Earley, P. (1993) Initiation Rights? Beginning Teachers Professional Development and the Objectives of Induction Training. Unpublished paper.

Earley, P. and Kinder, K. (1994) *Initiation Rights: Effective Induction Practices for New Teachers*. Slough: NFER.

Edwards, A. and Collison, J. (1996) *Mentoring and Developing Practice in Primary Schools: Supporting Student Teacher Learning in Schools*. Buckingham: Open University Press.

Edwards, A. D. (1978) The 'language of history' and the communication of historical knowledge, in A. K. Dickinson and P. J. Lee (eds) *History Teaching and Historical Understanding*. London: Heinemann.

Edwards, D. and Mercer, N. (1992) *Common Knowledge*. London, Routledge.

Elliott, B. and Calderhead, J. (1993) Mentoring for teacher development: possibilities and caveats, in D. McIntyre, H. Hagger and M. Wilkin (eds) *Mentoring: Perspectives on School Based Teacher Education*. London: Kogan Page.

Elliott, J. (1989) Appraisal: of performance or persons, in H. Simons and J. Elliott (eds) *Rethinking Appraisal and Assessment*. Buckingham: Open University Press.

Elliott, J. (ed.) (1995) *Reconstructing Teacher Education*. London: Falmer.

Elliott, J., McDonald, B., Argent, M. J., *et al*. (1986) *Police Probationer Training: The Final Report of the Stage II Review*. London: HMSO.

Eraut, M. (1994) *Developing Professional Knowledge and Competence*. London: Falmer.

Evans, A. (1994) Taking responsibility for the training curriculum within the school: the view of a professional tutor, in M. Wilkin and D. Sankey (eds) *Collaboration and Transition in Initial Teacher Training*. London: Kogan Page.

Feiman-Nemser, S., Parker, M. and Zeichner, K. (1993) Are mentor teachers teacher educators?, in D. McIntyre, H. Hagger and M. Wilkin (eds) *Mentoring: Perspectives on School Based Teacher Education*. London: Kogan Page.

Ferro, M. (1984) *The Use and Abuse of History: How the Past is Taught*. London: Routledge & Kegan Paul.

Fines, J. (1987) Making sense out of the content of the history curriculum, in C. Portal (ed.) *The History Curriculum for Teachers*. Lewes: Falmer.

Fullan, M. and Hargreaves, A. (eds) (1992) *Teacher Development and Educational Change*, London: Falmer.

Fullan, M. and Hargreaves, A. (1994) *What's Worth Fighting for in Your School?* Buckingham: Open University Press.

Fuller, F. F. and Brown, O. H. (1975) Becoming a teacher, in K. Ryan (ed.) *Teacher Education: The Seventy Fourth Year Book of the National Society for the Study of Education*. Chicago: University of Chicago Press.

Furlong, J. and Maynard, T. (1995) *Mentoring Student Teachers*. London: Routledge.

Furlong, V. J. (1995) Do Teachers need Universities? Inaugural lecture, University College of Wales Swansea.

Gardiner, H. (1992) Surprisingly disciplined squads, in K. Norman (ed.) *Thinking Voices: The Work of the National Oracy Project.* London: Hodder and Stoughton for the National Curriculum Council.

Giles, P. and Neal, G. (1983) History teaching analysed, in J. Fines (ed.) *Teaching History.* Edinburgh: Holmes McDougall.

Gilroy, D. P. (1992) Editorial: the political rape of teacher education in England and Wales – a JET rebuttal. *Journal of Education for Teaching,* 18(1): 5–22.

Gipps, C. (1996) The best tests in the world? or quality counts. *Research Intelligence,* 57: 23.

Graduate Teacher Training Registry (1996) *Annual Report.* London: Central Register and Clearing House.

Gray, J. (1996) Getting classroom value from value added research. *Research Intelligence,* 57: 22.

Gray, J. and Wilcox, B. (1995) *'Good School, Bad School': Evaluating Performance and Encouraging Improvement.* Buckingham: Open University Press.

Gudmundsdottir, S. (1988a) Curriculum stories, paper presented at the annual meeting of the International Study Association on Teacher Thinking.

Gudmundsdottir, S. (1988b) Managing the ideas: four case studies of high school teaching, paper presented at the annual meeting of the American Educational Research Association, New Orleans.

Gudmundsdottir, S. (1988c) Pedagogical content knowledge: expert–novice comparison in social studies, paper presented at the annual meeting of the American Educational Research Association, New Orleans.

Gudmundsdottir, S. (1991) Pedagogical models of subject matter, in J. Brophy (ed.) *Advances in Research on Teaching, Vol. 2.* Greenwich: JAI Press.

Gudmundsdottir, S. and Shulman, L. (1989) Pedagogical knowledge in social studies, in J. Lowyck and C. M. Clark (eds) *Teacher Thinking and Professional Action.* Leuven: Leuven University Press.

Guillame, A. M. and Rudney, G. L. (1993) Student teachers' growth towards independence: an analysis of their changing concerns. *Teaching and Teacher Education,* 9(1): 65–80.

Haggarty, L. (1996) *New Ideas for Teacher Education.* London: Cassell.

Hagger, H. (1997) Enabling student teachers to gain access to the professional craft knowledge of experienced teachers, in D. McIntyre (ed.) *Teacher Education Research in a New Context.* London: Paul Chapman.

Hagger, H., Burn, K. and McIntyre, D. (1995) *The School Mentor Handbook.* London: Kogan Page.

Hammersley, M. (1997) Educational research and teaching: a response to David Hargreaves' TTA lecture. *British Educational Research Journal,* 23(2): 141–61.

Hannam, C. (1981) *The First Year of Teaching.* Harmondsworth: Penguin.

Hargreaves, A. (1992) Cultures of teaching: a focus for change, in A. Hargreaves and M. Fullan (eds) *Understanding Teacher Development.* London: Cassell.

Hargreaves, A. and Fullan, M. G. (1992) *Understanding Teacher Development.* London: Cassell.

Hargreaves, D. (1996a) *Teaching as a Research-Based Profession: Possibilities and Prospects*. London: Teacher Training Agency.

Hargreaves, D. (1996b) Educational research and evidence-based educational practice: a response to critics. *Research Intelligence*, 58: 12–16.

Harris, S. and Rudduck, J. (1993) Establishing the seriousness of learning in the early years of secondary schooling. *British Journal of Educational Psychology*, 63: 322–36.

Harris, S. and Rudduck, J. (1995) 'School's great – apart from the lessons': students' early experiences of learning in secondary school, in M. Hughes (ed.) *Perceptions of Teaching and Learning*, BERA Dialogues 8. Clevedon: Multilingual Matters.

Helsby, G. (1996) Defining and developing professionalism in English secondary schools. *Journal of Education for Teaching*, 22(2): 135–48.

Hexter, J. H. (1972) *The History Primer*. London: Allen Lane.

Hill, D. (1995) The strong department: building the department as a learning community, in L. Santee Siskin and J. Warren Little (eds) *The Subjects in Question: Departmental Organisation and the High School*. New York: Teachers' College Press.

Hines, J. (1997) Raising students' performance in relation to NFER CAT scores, in Teacher Training Agency, *Teaching as a Research Based Profession: The Teacher Grant Scheme Summary of Findings*. London: TTA.

HMI (1985) *History in the Primary and Secondary Years*. London: HMSO.

HMI (1988) *The New Teacher in School: A Survey by HM Inspectors in England and Wales*. London: HMSO.

Howe, A. (1992) *Making Talk Work*. London: Hodder and Stoughton.

Huberman, M. (1989) On teachers' careers: once over lightly with a broad brush. *International Journal of Educational Research*, 13(4): 347–62.

Huberman, M. (1992) Teacher development and instructional mastery, in A. Hargreaves and M. Fullan (eds) *Understanding Teacher Development*. London: Cassell.

Husbands, C. (1992) Facing the facts: history in schools and the curriculum, in P. Black (ed.) *Education: Putting the Record Straight*. Stafford: Network Educational Press.

Husbands, C. (1996) *What is History Teaching? Language, Ideas and Meaning in Learning About the Past*. Buckingham: Open University Press.

Husbands, C. and Pendry, A. (1992) *Whose History? School History and the National Curriculum*. University of East Anglia: History Education Group.

Hustler, D. and McIntyre, D. (1996) *Developing Competent Teachers: Approaches to Professional Competence in Teacher Education*. London: David Fulton.

ILEA (1983) Language and History, in *History and Social Sciences at Secondary Level*, 2. London: ILEA. Reprinted in H. Bourdillon (1994) *Teaching History*. London: Routledge, for the Open University.

Jenkins, K. (1991) *Re-thinking History*. London: Routledge.

Jenkins, K. (1996) *On 'What is History?': From Carr and Elton to Rorty and White*. London: Routledge.

John, P. D. (1993) History tasks at Key Stage 3: a survey from five schools. *Teaching History*, 70: 18–21.

John, P. D. (1994) *Lesson Planning for Teachers*. London: Cassell.

Kagan, D. M. (1992) Professional growth among preservice and beginning teachers. *Review of Educational Research*, 62(2): 129–69.

Kerry, T. (1993) Evaluating INSET: the search for quality, in D. Bridges and T. Kerry (eds) *Developing Teachers Professionally*. London: Routledge.

Kerry, T. and Shelton-Mayes, A. (eds) (1995) *Issues in Mentoring*. London: Routledge.

Koestler, C. P. and Wubbels, J. P. (1995) Bridging the gap between initial teacher training and teacher induction. *Journal of Education for Teaching*, 21(3): 333–46.

Labbett, B. D. C. (1979) Towards a curriculum specification for history. *Journal of Curriculum Studies*, 11(2): 125–37.

Lacey, C. (1977) *The Socialization of Teachers*. London: Methuen.

Lee, P. (1991) Historical knowledge and the national curriculum, in R. Aldrich (ed.) *History in the National Curriculum*. London: Kogan Page.

Levine, N. (1981) *Language Teaching and Learning: History*. London: Ward Lock.

Levinson, D. J., Darrow, C. N., Klein, G. B., Levinson, M. H. and McKee, B. (1979) *The Seasons of a Man's Life*. New York: Knopf.

Lortie, D. C. (1975) *Schoolteacher: A Sociological Study*. Chicago: University of Chicago Press.

MacLennan, S. (1987) Integrating lesson planning and class management. *ELT Journal*, 41(3): 193–6.

Mahoney, P. and Hextall, I. (1997) *The Policy Context and Impact of the Teacher Training Agency: An ESRC Funded Project*. Roehampton Institute: Faculty of Education.

Marks, R. (1990) Pedagogical content knowledge: from a mathematical case to a modified conception. *Journal of Teacher Education*, 41(3): 3–11.

Martin, A. (ed.) (1992) *Teaching National Curriculum History with IT*. London: Historical Association for HABET.

Maynard, T. and Furlong, J. (1993) Learning to teach and models of mentoring, in D. McIntyre, H. Hagger and M. Wilkin (eds) *Mentoring: Perspectives on School Based Teacher Education*. London: Kogan Page.

McClelland, D. C. (1976) *A Guide to Job Competency Assessment*. Boston: McBer and Co.

McCulloch, M. and Fidler, B. (1994) *Improving Initial Teacher Training? New Roles for Teachers, Schools and Higher Education*. Harlow: Longman.

McDiarmid, G. W., Ball, D. and Anderson, C. (1989) Why staying one chapter ahead doesn't really work: subject specific pedagogy, in M. C. Reynolds (ed.) *Knowledge Base for the Beginning Teacher*. Oxford: Pergamon.

McGill, J. (1988) In the history classroom, in J. Hickman and K. Kimberley (eds) *Teachers, Language and Learning*. London: Routledge.

McIntyre, D. (1990) The Oxford Internship and the Cambridge analytical framework: two models of teacher education, in M. B. Booth, V. J. Furlong and M. Wilkin (eds) *Partnership in Initial Teacher Training*. London: Cassell.

McIntyre, D. (1994) Classrooms and learning environments for student teachers, in M. Wilkin and D. Sankey (eds), *Collaboration and Transition in Initial Teacher Training*. London: Kogan Page.

McIntyre, D. and Hagger, H. (1992) Professional development through the Oxford Internship model. *British Journal of Educational Studies* XXXX(3): 264–83.

McIntyre, D. and Hagger, H. (1993) Teachers' expertise and models of mentoring, in D. McIntyre, H. Hagger and M. Wilkin (eds) *Mentoring: Perspectives on School Based Teacher Education*. London: Kogan Page.

McKiernan, H. (1993) History in a national curriculum: imagining the nation at the end of the twentieth century. *Journal of Curriculum Studies*, 25(1): 33–51.

Millet, A. (1996) *Pedagogy: The Last Corner of the Secret Garden*. London: University of London, King's College.

Moon, B. and Shelton-Mayes, A. (1995) Frameworks, competences and quality: open learning dimensions to initial teacher education and training, in H. Bines and J. M. Welton (eds) *Managing Partnership in Teacher Training and Development*. London: Routledge.

Morine-Dershimer, G. (1979) Teacher plan and classroom reality: the South Bay Study Part 4. Research monograph. MI: Institute for Research on Teaching, University of Michigan.

Morris, C. (1992) Opening doors: learning history through talk, in T. Booth, W. Swann, M. Masterton and P. Potts (eds) *Learning for All, 1: Curricula for Diversity in Education*. London: Routledge.

Myers, K. (1996) *School Improvement in Practice: Schools Make a Difference Project*. Lewes: Falmer.

Neelands, J. (1993) *Learning Through Imagined Experience: The Role of Drama in the National Curriculum*. London: Hodder and Stoughton.

Norman, K. (1992) *Thinking Voices: The Work of the National Oracy Project*. London: Hodder and Stoughton for the National Curriculum Council.

Norris, N. (1991) The trouble with competence. *Cambridge Journal of Education*, 21(3): 331–5.

Ofsted (1993) *The New Teacher in School: A Survey by HM Inspectors in England and Wales 1992*. London: HMSO.

Ofsted (1994) *Improving Schools*. London: HMSO.

Ofsted (1995) *History: A Review of Inspection Findings 1993–4*. London: HMSO.

Ofsted (1996) *Subjects and Standards*. London: HMSO.

Ofsted (1997a) *From Failure to Success: How Special Measures are Helping Schools to Improve*. London: HMSO.

Ofsted (1997b) *Subject Management in Secondary Schools*. London: HMSO.

O'Sullivan, F., Jones, K. and Reid, K. (1997) The development of staff, in L. Kydd, M. Crawford and C. Riches (eds) *Professional Development for Educational Management*. Buckingham: Open University Press.

Pendry, A. (1981) *The Significance of Teaching History as a Body of Knowledge or as a Method of Study*. MA dissertation, Institute of Education, University of London.

Pendry, A. (1990) Dilemmas for history teacher educators. *British Journal of Educational Studies*, xxxviii(1): 47–62.

Pendry, A. and O'Neill, C. (1997) Research agendas and history teacher educators, in A. Pendry and C. O'Neill (eds) *Principles and Practice*. Lancaster: SCHTE.

Pendry, A. E. (1994) 'The pre-lesson pedagogigcal decision-making of history student teachers during the internship year', unpublished PhD thesis. University of Oxford.

Pendry, A. E. (1997) The pedagogical thinking and learning of history student teachers, in D. McIntyre (ed.) *Teacher Education Research in a New Context*. London: Paul Chapman.

Pendry, A., Atha, J., Carden, S., Courtenay, L., Keogh, C. and Ruston, K. (1997) Pupil preconceptions in history. *Teaching History*, 86(Jan.): 18–20.

Phillips, R. (1993) Teachers' perceptions on the first year's implementation of Key Stage 3 history in the National Curriculum in England. *Research Papers in Education*, 8(3): 329–53.

Phillips, R. (1997) National identity and history teaching in Britain: English, Northern Irish, Scottish and Welsh perspectives, in A. Pendry and C. O'Neill (eds) *Principles and Practice: Analytical Perspectives on Curriculum Reform and Changing Pedagogy from History Teacher Educators*. Lancaster: SCHTE.

Portal, C. (ed.) (1987) *Sources in History: From Definition to Assessment*. Eastleigh: SREB.

Postlethwaite, K. (1993) *Differentiated Science Teaching*. Buckingham: Open University Press.

Price, M. (1968) History in danger. *History*, 53: 342–7.

Riley, M. (1997) Big stories and big pictures: making outlines and overviews interesting. *Teaching History*, 88: 20–22.

Robertson, J. (1981) *Effective Classroom Control*. London: Hodder and Stoughton.

Rothwell, S., Nardi, E. and McIntyre, D. (1994) The perceived values of the role activities of mentors, curricular, professional and general tutors, in I. Reid, H. Constable and R. Griffiths (eds) *Teacher Education Reform: Current Research*. London: Paul Chapman.

Rovegno, I. (1992) Learning a new curricular approach: mechanisms of knowledge acquisition in preservice teachers. *Teaching and Teacher Education*, 8(3): 253–64.

Rudduck, J., Chaplain, R. and Wallace, G. (1996) *School Improvement: What Can Pupils Tell Us?* London: David Fulton.

Sanders, S. (1994) Mathematics and mentoring, in B. Jaworski and A. Watson (eds) *Mentoring in Mathematics Teaching*. London: Falmer.

Satterly, D. (1989) *Assessment in Schools*. Oxford: Blackwell.

SCAA (1997) *Extended Writing in Key Stage 3 History, Discussion Papers no. 8*. London: SCAA.

SCDC (1989) *The National Writing Project*. London: SCDC.

Schama, S. (1992) *Dead Certainties: Unwarranted Speculations*. London: Granta Books.

Schön, D. A. (1983) *The Reflective Practitioner: How Professionals Think in Action*. New York: Basic Books.

Schön, D. A. (1987) *Educating the Reflective Practitioner*. London: Jossey-Bass Publications.

Schools Council History 13–16 Project (1976) *A New Look at History.* Edinburgh: Holmes McDougall.

Schostak, J. F. and Phillips, T. J. (1995) *Assessing Competences in Nurse Education: The Report of the ACE Project.* Norwich: University of East Anglia.

Shaw, R. (1992) *Teacher Training in Secondary Schools.* London: Kogan Page.

Sheeran, Y. and Barnes, D. (1991) *School Writing: Discovering the Ground Rules.* Buckingham: Open University Press.

Shemilt, D. (1980) *History 13–16: Evaluation Study.* Edinburgh: Holmes McDougall.

Shemilt, D. (1987) Adolescent ideas about evidence and methodology in history, in C. Portal (ed.) *The History Curriculum for Teachers.* Lewes: Falmer.

Sikes, P. (1985) The life cycle of the teacher, in S. J. Ball and I. F. Goodson (eds) *Teachers' Lives and Careers.* Lewes: Falmer.

Sikes, P. (1997) *Parents as Teachers.* London: Cassell.

Siskin, L. S. and Little, J. W. (1995) *The Subjects in Question.* New York: Teachers' College Press.

Skidelsky, R. (1988) History as social engineering. *The Independent,* 1 March 1988.

Slater, J. (1989) The politics of history teaching: a humanity dehumanised? Special professorial lecture, University of London Institute of Education.

Slater, J. (1995) *Teaching History in the New Europe.* London: Cassell.

Somekh, B., Altrichter, H. and Posch, P. (1994) *Teachers Investigate their Practice.* London: Routledge.

Spencer, A. (1995) In mid career, in J. Bell (ed.) *Teachers Talk About Teaching: Coping with Change in Turbulent Times.* Buckingham: Open University Press.

SREB (1986) *Empathy in History: from Definition to Assessment.* Eastleigh: SREB.

Steffy, B. (1989) *Career Stages of Classroom Teachers.* Lancaster, Penn: Technomic Publishing Inc. Co.

Stenhouse, L. (1978) Cultures, attitudes and education. *Royal Society of Arts Journal,* CXXVI: 735–45.

Stronach, I., Cope, P., Inglis, B. and McNally, J. (1996) 'Competence' Guidelines in Scotland for Initial Teacher Training: 'Supercontrol' or 'superperformance'? in D. Hustler and D. McIntyre (eds) *Developing Competent Teachers.* London: David Fulton.

Sutherland, S. (1997) Report 10: Teaching education and training: a study, in National Commission of Inquiry into Higher Education. *Higher Education in the Learning Society.* London: NCIHE.

Sutton, C. (1992) *Words, Science and Learning.* Buckingham: Open University Press.

Sylvester, D. (1994) Change and continuity in history teaching, 1900–1993, in H. Bourdillon (ed.) *Teaching History.* London: Routledge for the Open University.

Tate, N. (1995) Speech to the Council of Europe Conference on the role of history in the formation of national identity York, 18 September.

Teacher Training Agency (1997) *Teaching as a Research Based Profession: The Teacher Grant Scheme Summary of Findings.* London: TTA.

Tickle, L. (1994) *The Induction of New Teachers: Reflective Professional Practice.* London: Cassell.

Tomlinson, P. (1995) *Understanding Mentoring: Reflective Strategies for School-Based Teacher Preparation.* Buckingham: Open University Press.

Turner, T. with Field, K. and Arthur, J. (1997) Working with your mentor, in S. Capel, M. Leask and T. Turner (eds) *Starting to Teach in the Secondary School.* London: Routledge.

Visram, R. (1994) British history; whose history? Black perspectives on British history, in H. Bourdillon (ed.) *Teaching History.* London: Routledge.

Vygotsky, L. (1987) *The Collected Works of L. S. Vygotsky, Volume 1.* London: Plenum.

Waterhouse, P. (1985) *Managing the Learning Process.* London and New York: McGraw-Hill.

Whitty, G. (1996) Professional competences and professional characteristics: the Northern Ireland approach to the reform of teacher education, in D. Hustler and D. McIntyre (eds) *Developing Competent Teachers.* London: David Fulton.

Wilcox, B. and Gray, J. (1996) *Inspecting Schools: Holding Schools to Account and Helping Schools to Improve.* Buckingham: Open University Press.

Wilkin, M. (1996) *Initial Teacher Training: The Dialogue of Ideology and Culture.* Lewes: Falmer.

Williams, A. (1993) Teacher perceptions of their needs as mentors in the context of developing school-based initial teacher education. *British Educational Research Journal,* 19(4): 407–20.

Williams, A. (ed.) (1994) *Perspectives on Partnership.* London: Falmer.

Wilson, S. M. (1989) Understanding historical understanding: an analysis of the subject matter knowledge of teachers, paper presented at the annual meeting of the American Educational Research Association, San Francisco.

Wilson, S. M. (1990a) History as context: how does it shed light on teaching? Unpublished paper.

Wilson, S. M. (1990b) Mastadons, maps and Michigan: exploring uncharted territory while teaching elementary social studies. Meeting paper, presented at the annual meeting of the American Educational Research Association, Boston, annual meeting.

Wilson, S. M. and Wineburg, S. S. (1988) Peering at history through different lenses: the role of disciplinary perspectives in teaching history. *Teachers College Record,* 89(4): 525–41.

Wineburg, S. S. (1991a) Historical problem solving: a study of the cognitive processes used in the evaluation of documentary and pictorial evidence. *Journal of Educational Psychology,* 83(1): 73–87.

Wineburg, S. S. (1991b) On the reading of historical texts: notes on the breach between school and academy. Unpublished paper.

Wineburg, S. S. and Wilson, S. M. (1988a) Subject matter knowledge in the teaching of history. Unpublished paper.

Wineburg, S. S. and Wilson, S. M. (1988b) Models of wisdom in the teaching of History. *Phi Delta Kappan,* 70: 50–8.

Wragg, E. C. and Brown, G. (1993) *Explaining*. London: Routledge.

Wragg, E. C., Wragg, C., Wikeley, F. J. and Haynes, G. S. (1996) *Teacher Appraisal Observed*. London: Routledge.

Wray, D. and Lewis, M. (1994) *Developing Children's Non-Fiction Writing – Working with Writing Frames*. Leamington Spa: Scholastic.

Wynn, B. (1994) Partnership – a headteacher's view, in A. Williams (ed.) *Perspectives on Partnership*. London: Falmer.

Zeichner, K. M. (1993) Traditions of practice in US preservice teacher education programs. *Teaching and Teacher Education*, 9(1): 1–13.

Zeichner, K. M. and Liston, D. P. (1987) Teaching student teachers to reflect. *Harvard Educational Review*, 57(1): 23–48.

INDEX

EFFECTIVE TEACHING AND LEARNING
TEACHERS' AND STUDENTS' PERSPECTIVES

Paul Cooper and Donald McIntyre

This book examines how teachers and students *actually* go about their classroom business. It carefully avoids the assumptions of policy-makers and theorists about what *ought* to be happening and focuses on what *is* happening. In doing so, the authors offer:

- a detailed look at how teachers are responding to the National Curriculum
- a unique insight into secondary school students as learners
- a grounded analysis of teaching and learning strategies drawing on the psychological theories of Bruner and Vygotsky.

The book follows on from Donald McIntyre's previous book *Making Sense of Teaching* and will be of interest to student teachers, teachers studying for advanced degrees and academics involved in teacher education.

Contents
Exploring classroom strategies for effective teaching and learning – Gaining access to teachers' and pupils' thinking: problems, principles and processes – The National Curriculum context – Teachers' craft knowledge – Pupils' craft knowledge compared with that of teachers – Interactions between teacher and pupil craft knowledge – Catering for individual differences between pupils – The crafts of the classroom – References – Author index – Subject index.

192pp   0 335 19379 X (Paperback)   0 335 19380 3 (Hardback)

WHAT IS HISTORY TEACHING?
LANGUAGE, IDEAS AND MEANING IN LEARNING ABOUT THE PAST

Chris Husbands

Any teacher of history, from primary school to
university, can learn much from this articulate book.

Richard Brown

- How do pupils make sense of the past?
- What is the relationship between the way historians construct interpretations of the past and the way pupils learn history in schools?

This book draws together developments in a wide range of fields: in academic history, in the study of language and in classroom research on pupil learning, as the basis for a distinctive approach to the teaching and learning of history in school. Chris Husbands analyses four approaches to learning about the past, through story and through the imagination. He emphasizes the ways in which pupils and historians structure their own interpretations of history and considers the implications for teachers by examining the ways in which classroom talk, writing and assessment can support the development of sophisticated understandings of the past.

Contents
Preface – Part 1: Understanding history – Introduction: learning from the past – Understanding the past: evidence and questions – Understanding the past: language and change – Historical forms: narratives and stories – Historical forms: facts, fictions and imagination – Part 2: History in the classroom – Understandings and misunderstandings – Ways of talking: words, classrooms and history – Organizing ideas: the place of writing – Making judgements – So, what is history teaching? – Bibliography – Index.

160pp   0 335 19638 1 (Paperback)   0 335 19639 X (Hardback)

THE GOOD MENTOR GUIDE
INITIAL TEACHER EDUCATION IN SECONDARY SCHOOLS

Val Brooks and Pat Sikes

Recent changes in educational policy have resulted in schools taking on greater responsibility for initial teacher education. This means that, increasingly, school teachers are being called upon to adopt the role of mentor and to provide professional and subject guidance and supervision for student teachers.

This book addresses issues which concern secondary school teachers in their new role as mentors:

- What does good practice in mentoring look like?
- What strategies exist for managing mentoring?
- How should mentors deal with assessment issues?

By combining both theoretical and practical aspects of mentoring and by providing rich case studies of real life situations, this book offers much needed support to mentors. It will be invaluable to new mentors and will also provide a useful resource for the professional development of existing mentors.

Contents
Introduction – The context of mentoring – Exploring some models of mentoring – Roles and responsibilities – Managing mentoring – Working with students – Assessment – Becoming a more effective mentor – Appendix circular no 9/92: initial teacher training (secondary phase) – References – Index.

192pp   0 335 19758 2 (Paperback)   0 335 19759 0 (Hardback)